A PORTRAIT OF A PITTSBURGH

MILLHUNKS

AND

RENEGADES

ANITA KULINA

BRANDT
STREET
PRESS

"Millhunks and Renegades:
A Portrait of a Pittsburgh Neighborhood"

by Anita Kulina

© 2003 by Anita Kulina

Second Printing, 2004

Published by
Brandt Street Press
P. O. Box 8243
Pittsburgh, PA 15217-0243
www.brandtstreetpress.com

ISBN 0-9742607-3-8

CIP 2003107522

Cover and Book Design by
Mike Murray
Pearhouse Productions
7033 Meade Place #1
Pittsburgh, PA 15208
412-244-8698
www.pearhouse.com

Printed in the United States of America

A Note to the Reader

Italicized quoted material was collected during interviews with the people on page 159. Those interviewed range in age from 12 to 96. Most are or were residents of Greenfield; others were interviewed because of their unique knowledge of events that impacted the area. They included steelworkers, housewives, professionals in various fields, schoolchildren, historical re-enactors and descendants of pioneer families.

Quotes are not attributed to individuals. This was done in agreement with those interviewed to protect their privacy, giving them the opportunity to be more candid in their remarks. Also to ensure privacy, names have been replaced with "my husband," "my sister," etc. I trust that this technique will not interfere with your enjoyment of the story. ◆

To my Mum,
who always told me I can
go anywhere in a book.

Contents

What it used to be   What it is now

Allegheny City	North Side
Ayers Hill	Duquesne University Campus
Black Bear Town	Coshocton, Ohio
Braddock's Field Path	Second Avenue
Coal Hill	Mount Washington
Diondega	The Point
Garrison Street	Lydia Street
Girty's Run	Millvale, Pennsylvania
Girty's Town	St. Mary's, Ohio
Graphic Street	Kish Way
Logstown	Economy, Pennsylvania
Mary Street	Alger Street
Mount Airy	Hill near Bigelow & Lydia Streets
Pittsburgh Pirates	Pittsburgh Steelers
Roosevelt School	Greenfield Giant Eagle
St. Rosalia Convent	GO Center
Salt Lick Road	Saline Street
Shannopin's Town	Lawrenceville
Slag Dump	Century III Mall
Stringtown	East Liberty
Squirrel Hill Road	Bigelow Street
Tunsel Hill	Hill near Bigelow & Lydia Streets
Virgin Alley	Oliver Avenue
Wheatland Avenue	McCaslin Street

GREENFIELD

reenfield is a neighborhood in the East End section of Pittsburgh, Pennsylvania, bordered by the neighborhoods of Squirrel Hill and Hazelwood. The city of Pittsburgh defines Greenfield's boundaries as Saline Street to the east and west, Hazelwood Avenue and Bigelow Street to the south and the Penn-Lincoln Parkway to the north. ◆

IT ALL BEGAN WITH A GLACIER

Long before there was a Western Pennsylvania, an ancient glacier cut its path over the land. It left a lake, and over time this lake became finger lakes. The finger lakes became rivers. Rivers wound through lush valleys we now call by names like Edgewood, Wilkinsburg, East Liberty, Panther Hollow, Oakland and Bloomfield.

The rivers, over time, gave birth to runs—lively streams that fed the valleys and wove the rivers to the land. This is the story of one of those streams, Four Mile Run, and the town that grew around it. ♦

PROLOGUE

The first visitors to the hills and valleys we call Western Pennsylvania were ancient Indians. They came south along Alaska's frozen Bering Strait, making their way though all types of terrain on their quest for a better land in which to live. They found it in a vast, green forest, thick with beech, chestnut, maple and oak trees that reached from bank to bank of lush river valleys. Building villages on hilltops along the Monongahela River, their round houses huddled together in a snug circle, they surrounded their settlement with mounds of earth. No one is really sure what the earth mounds were for, but scholars speculate the Indians used them to track the path of the sun so they could plan the best times to sow seeds and to harvest.

The women of these tribes were probably the first farmers on the continent. They spent their days working fields of beans, corn, sunflowers and squash, while little children played and men fished or hunted the abundant wild game that lived throughout the deep forests.

Century after century, tribes of Mound Builders came and went through the Ohio Valley. Those who arrived later to settle in the forest along the rivers constructed earthen mounds to mark their territory, as their grandfathers did before them. They also built smaller mounds to bury their dead, and each time they visited the grave of a loved one, they added a stone to the mound. Over years and generations, some of these mounds grew to enormous proportions.

Severe droughts eventually forced the Mound Builders east and south in search of new farming lands. After they were gone, the river valley they had called home was inhabited only by beasts and birds for a long time. ◆

Stones from Indian mounds built along Four Mile Run in Greenfield and on what became Mansion Street in Hazelwood were used to pave the old Indian trail that became Second Avenue.

It's estimated that there are 10,000 Indian mounds in the Ohio Valley.

1 | TRIBES, TRAPPERS AND TRADERS

By the time the 17th century arrived, wildlife was scarce in Europe since most of the animals had been killed to supply fur hats and coats for the aristocracy. Now these wealthy Europeans needed a new supply of fur. Traders crossed the ocean to the wilderness of North America in search of fresh game and hunters to provide it.

The Indians of the Iroquois Federation—also known as the Six Nations—lived along America's northern Atlantic coast and were happy to trade fur pelts for European goods. In fact, it wasn't long before the Iroquois depleted the animal life in their own territory and needed fresh hunting grounds themselves. They got it the easiest way they knew how, by seizing the land of their neighbors, the Lenape Indians. By the end of the Iroquois-Susquehannock War, the Delaware River Valley was Iroquois territory, and the Lenape, who had lived along the Delaware River for thousands of years, were escorted west. Seneca Indians from the Six Nations led them across the Appalachian Mountains to join the Shawnee Indians in the thick forests along the rivers in the Ohio Valley.

The Iroquois Federation, also called the Six Nations, included the Cayuga, Mohawk, Oneida, Onondaga, Seneca and Tuscarora tribes. The name Iroquois refers to the language they spoke.

Traders named the river near the Lenape camp "Delaware" after Lord de la Warr, the governor of the colony of Virginia.

INDIAN TRIBES THAT LIVED OR HUNTED
IN WESTERN PENNSYLVANIA

Cherokee	Miami	Pottowatami
Cornplanter	Mynoje	Seneca
Lenape	Ojibwe	Shawnee
		Wyandot

The Long Knives, the European frontiersmen who traded with the Indians, called this tribe the Delaware, but the Indians called themselves Lenape, which means "original people." Indians who spoke the Algonquin language believed the Lenape were their "grandfathers," the tribe from which they had all descended. The Shawnee spoke Algonquin, so when the Lenape arrived at their new home along the Ohio River, they were treated with due respect. The Seneca, on the other hand, were Iroquois and so considered themselves rulers over the other two tribes. Iroquois chiefs presided over the valley, with Guyasuta as governor or "half-king" and Queen Aliquippa as ruler of a village along the river.

The Lenape, Shawnee and Seneca lived peacefully in the river valley, and sometimes different tribes even lived and worked together in the same village. The Indians named the rivers that ran through their forests, calling them "falling-in banks" or Menaugehilla (Monongahela) and "beautiful water," O-y-o (Ohio). When they had business with neighboring tribes, the Indians met at the point where the rivers meet, a place they called Diondega.

There was enough wildlife to feed everyone in these lush forests, especially four miles up the Monongahela River from Diondega in the area that later became known as Four Mile Run. A natural deposit of salt at the base of this creek guaranteed that game was plentiful and hunting effortless. Lenape, Shawnee and Seneca men speared fish or caught them in snares. While they hunted, the women tilled the rich soil along the river banks. Their farms—some as large as two hundred acres—overflowed with sweet potatoes, tobacco, beans, corn and squash. They tapped maple trees for sugar in the springtime and filled woven baskets with wild apples, berries and nuts in the fall. Every house had its own root cellar, a storage pit where foods were kept for the winter. Families gathered together for dinners of boiled game and vegetables served up in pottery bowls with spoons made from elk antlers.

At first glance, it wasn't easy for the Long Knives to tell the Lenape, Shawnee and Seneca apart. People from all three tribes were as tall as the Long Knives, but built more like athletes. Their dark eyes looked out of brown faces with straight noses and high cheekbones. Everyone except the warriors had long, straight black hair; warriors wore their hair

Queen Aliquippa's Indian village was in McKees Rocks.

Four Mile Run followed the course of what is now Saline Street. The street was named for the salt lick at the base of the creek.

An acre is about the size of a football field.

Flocks of passenger pigeons were sometimes so thick they covered the sky like clouds.

A scalplock is often called a Mohawk but actually was worn by many tribes in the east.

A piece of wampum was a tubular bead made from a shell.

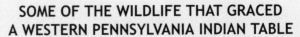

SOME OF THE WILDLIFE THAT GRACED A WESTERN PENNSYLVANIA INDIAN TABLE				
GAME				
bear	deer	marten	pigeon	turkey
beaver	elk	mink	rabbit	weasel
cougar	fisher	otter	squirrel	wolf
FISH				
bass	brook trout	catfish	pike	sturgeon

in a scalplock. Men wore deerskin breechcloths, and women wore deerskin skirts. Children sometimes didn't wear any clothes at all. But each tribe had its own distinct culture and, if you knew what to look for, differences were easy to spot.

Lenape women pierced their ears and rouged their cheeks with bloodroot or burnt ochre. Lenape men and women decorated themselves with tattoos. They lived in wigwams and traveled in dugout canoes.

The Lenape were respectful of women. In their tribes, women owned the houses, and any children borne to a marriage were considered to belong to their mother's clan. Women spoke up when tribal leaders made decisions on whether and when to wage war. If prisoners were taken, sometimes it was the women who chose which to adopt and which should suffer a harsher fate.

Some of the Lenape settlements scattered throughout the Ohio River Valley were Moravian missions. The Moravians were a religious group from Germany who left the Lutheran church hoping to create what they considered "true" Christian communities. They traveled to South Africa and the West Indies, converting slaves to Christianity, before they came to the frontier of America. When the Lenape were forced to leave the Delaware Valley, Moravian missionaries followed. Lenape Christian communities sprang up along the Ohio River, where the Indians made crafts to sell and lived a quiet, peaceful life.

Though there were quite a few of these Moravian settlements, most of the Lenape kept the religion of their forefathers. Lenape priests were healers, or seers who told the future and interpreted dreams. The Lenape religion forbade using real names outside the tribe, so the Lenape instead went by nicknames when trading with the Long Knives. An important Lenape chief whose real name meant "maker of daylight" went by the nickname Hopocan, which means "tobacco pipe," so the Long Knives called him Captain Pipe. Both traditional and Christian Lenape believed in an afterlife, and neither believed in heaven or hell.

The word Shawnee means "southerner." The name comes from the fact that the Shawnee homeland in the Ohio Valley was south of the homeland of the Great Lakes tribes. Shawnee legend had it that, although descended from the Lenape, their people were originally from Cuba.

Since the Shawnee were often driven from their homes by war, much of their culture was nomadic. They spent summers in bark-covered longhouses in the village, but winter would find them scattered about in smaller hunting camps. While all the Indians were wearing fur coats with their deerskin jackets and pants, the Shawnee turned theirs inside-out so the warm fur was next to their skin.

To recognize the Seneca, on the other hand, you would need to know that their men and women had pierced noses and wore a nose-ring that dangled a small shell or a piece of wampum. The Seneca, whose name means "people of the big hill," lived in bark-covered longhouses.

Their culture had a respect for women similar to that of the Lenape. In the Seneca culture, both men and women could be priests. Their priests taught that there was a Great Creator who lived in the sky and watched over them. This Great Creator had come to earth a long time ago as the son of a virgin, bringing a message of peace.

The Seneca were also called Mingo.

John Frazier's trading post was in the area now known as Braddock.

The Seneca believed that all nature's creations, even hills and storms, had a soul or inner spirit. A person's inner spirit was so valuable to the tribe that, if they were killed, another person needed to be adopted to take their place.

There were customs shared by all three tribes. Elderly Indians were treated with great respect. Young children were not spoiled, but they were never beaten either—a shock of cold water and tales of reprimands from ghosts in the night were usually enough to keep a wayward scamp in line. Marriages were arranged by parents, though the young couple was allowed to voice their opinion of the potential mate. Divorce, though acceptable, was very rare.

Frenchmen traded goods for animal pelts with the Indians along the Ohio River, and John Frazier ran the valley's trading post. Despite the many cultural differences between the Indians and the Europeans—one being the fact that the traders did not have the scrupulous attendance to personal hygiene that the Indians did—the Indians were friendly to the French. Since Indian tradition was to trade only among family, many traders married Indian women. French traders and Indians often spent evenings together in diversions like cards and dice, wrestling or lacrosse—always with a friendly bet riding on the outcome.

Now strong steel knives replaced the Indians's bone knives, and food was cooked in iron and brass vessels instead of clay pots. Hunting was faster and easier with the European firearms. Leisure changed, for good or for bad, with the use of rum, much stronger than the beer the Indians made.

Trading required travel, mostly by canoe on the rivers. Inland travel, when necessary, meant an intricate web of trails—so many that, if someone got lost, it was often because there were too many tracks to follow. Trails tended to stretch along high ridges, since high ground was windswept clean of snow in winter and sun-dried after summer rains. But if the high ground didn't reach all the way to a destination, there were plenty of low-lying trails along the banks of the rivers and runs.

The most traveled path near Four Mile Run was Nemacolin's Path, blazed by an Indian named Nemacolin and a settler named Michael Cresap who lived along the trail. Nemacolin's Path reached west from the Potomac River to Diondega where the Monongahela River meets the Ohio. A traveler to Diondega often saved a few hours on his journey by taking one of the shortcuts through Four Mile Run.

These trails were maintained only by their travelers, so the way was often covered with vegetation or blocked with trees and branches that fell during a storm. Heavily traveled paths were sprinkled with shelters every ten miles or so, some built specifically for travelers, others left behind from deserted Indian villages. A typical cabin was nine feet by six feet, open-sided, with the roof higher in the front than in the back so the rain and snow could slide off. If there was no shelter, a few men might band together to quickly put up a cabin for the night, usually in an open area near water and grass for the horses. Shelters were often well known to travelers and called by colorful names such as "Cock's Eye Cabin" or "Old King Nutimus."

A journey to trade, visit relatives or sign a treaty meant a walking trip that lasted for days. Indians, traders, hunters and express riders all used these trails, and it was a common sight to find hunters sharing a meal with a trader while they caught up on the latest news, or an express rider smoking a pipe with a group of Indians before bedding down for the night. Pictures painted on trees with charcoal and red ochre displayed the latest Indian news of successful hunts or war parties. Near a Moravian mission, travelers might pass Bible verses painted on trees by the Lenape.

Toward the middle of the 18th century, the British asked the Iroquois for permission to build a British trading post at Diondega. When the Iroquois agreed, the British understood this to mean that Diondega and the land surrounding it now belonged to Britain.

A group of men in the British colony of Virginia created the Ohio Land Company to develop and colonize the Ohio River Valley.

Traders and trappers from Europe had already begun to trickle across the Appalachians to the West. Some were folks who had been recruited from Germany and Northern Ireland by William Penn to people Pennsylvania, his "Holy Experiment," then were kicked out for violating Penn's strict rules forbidding vice of any kind. Others were runaways, Scots who had been taken prisoner by the British in a Scottish revolt and shipped to America to work out their prison terms as indentured servants. And now Virginia wanted to send more settlers to Iroquois land.

Everyone was disturbed at this news. The Indians had no problem with French traders, who traveled through and built a house here and there, but seemed to have no interest in creating French colonies in the Ohio Valley. But the concept of land ownership was completely foreign to Indians, who felt that land belonged to the Great Creator and could not be owned by men. And these new folks claimed to own the land.

Word of the Ohio Land Company traveled to Philadelphia. To prevent Virginia from cutting into Pennsylvania's lucrative fur trade, Pennsylvanians sent their own representative, George Croghan, to meet with the Indians at Logstown and set up a trading post along the Ohio River.

The French were most nervous about this new British presence in the West. The Catholic French had considered the British to be heretics ever since Britain's Henry VIII left the Catholic Church to create the Church of England and demanded that all his subjects worship there. Back in Europe, it looked like war between the British and the French would start any day. The French in America were not so quick to want war for the simple reason that they were vastly outnumbered. There were 200,000 British in Pennsylvania alone, never mind all the other British colonies, and only 55,000 French in the whole of Canada.

French traders had considered the Ohio River territory theirs for trade for a hundred years now, ever since LaSalle and a couple of priests made the first trip through the area. French colonies in Louisiana and Canada could not afford to lose access to the rivers at the hands of the British. Somehow, the French needed to protect themselves. Captain Louis Celeron de Bienville was sent downriver to the Delaware village of Shannopin's Town to bury a series of lead plates along the Ohio River that would claim the area for France.

Virginia soon got wind of this strategy. Two of the organizers of the Ohio Land Company, Lawrence and John Washington, sent their younger brother George, a 21-year-old surveyor, to claim the land they felt was rightfully theirs. George rode along Nemacolin's Path with a small group of Virginians and a few Indian guides. They traveled to the forest at the forks of the river and then on to Fort Le Boeuf, 17 miles south of Lake Erie's Presque Isle. The French greeted them and politely but firmly told Washington that they had already claimed the Ohio River, and Virginia had no rights to it.

Trouble was brewing. ♦

Since European settlements, including Pennsylvania, were along the east coast, any place west of the Appalachian Mountains was considered "The West."

Areas near Pittsburgh that had settlers during this period included Munhall, North Side, Oakland and Wilkinsburg.

Captain Louis Celeron de Bienville's route went past the area now known as Pittsburgh's Highland Park.

Shannopin's Town is now called Lawrenceville.

2

KIDNAPPED!

The Girty homestead was northeast of Harrisburg, Pennsylvania. Lancaster County at this time was much larger and included this area.

Among the many adventurers who came to America to seek their fortune was a rough-and-tumble Irishman named Simon Girty. As he crossed the ocean toward the new land, though it's a cinch he never suspected that his sons would be early settlers of Greenfield, it probably would have come as no surprise to Girty that his boys would grow up to be some of the first notorious outlaws of the American West.

When Simon Girty arrived in America, he met and married Mary Newton, a young English girl half his age. With their four young sons—Thomas, Simon Jr., James and George—they set up a homestead on 300 acres of land in Lancaster County. Girty went into the trading business, traveling north to buy goods at Thomas McKee's trading post and then bringing them back to sell to the Indians. Mary stayed home with the boys.

Sometimes Girty traveled alone, sometimes with his partner, John Turner. It was a long walk over rough terrain, their packhorse team trudging single file with one man guiding in front and another behind. If folks were traveling, Girty and Turner were men to avoid.

Simon Sr. was not a nice man. He was a drinker, and he had a hot temper.

Consider the time they ran into a Delaware Indian known as Fish. The Indian had furs to swap, but all their trade goods had already been bartered. Instead, they took Fish to Chamber's Mill and got him drunk. The next day, Fish's body was in the mill pond and his furs were on the back of Turner's packhorse.

Girty often came home from a few days on the trail with a belly full of rum and a half-dozen Indians. The Girty home always seemed to be full to the brim with people. Simon Girty, Mary and the boys, John Turner, and their indentured servant Honour Edwards all lived there, and when you added Girty's guests, it made for a houseful.

Mary and the boys weren't welcome in the homes of their German neighbors because of Simon's Indian friends and his loud ways, but the Girty boys never seemed to mind. Their Indian guests brought gifts,

played games with them and gave them the attention they never got from their father.

Simon Girty was murdered not long after George was born. Town gossip said it happened during a drunken brawl. Girty and Samuel Sanders, the British officer who killed him, may have been drunk, but the confrontation—folks said they were fighting over Mary Girty—was a full-fledged duel. The men started with guns and, when both of them missed each other, moved on to swords. Sanders ran Girty through, and the soldier was taken to jail and convicted of manslaughter.

Mary took up with John Turner, and they had a son they named John Jr. Turner, now head of the family, sold the Girty homestead and took his charges along the Juniata River to Old Indian Town. They were just in time to help the British build Fort Granville to defend themselves against the Indians and the French. Turner built his new family a cabin near the fort.

John Turner sold the Girty homestead to John Harris, who later founded Harrisburg.

Forts were going up fast and furiously because things were getting heated in Pennsylvania. There were British blockades stopping the flow of trade from Canada, so the French were losing connection with their Indian allies. The blockade meant more opportunities for other traders, and everybody and his brother seemed to be trying to cash in on the action. Now the Seneca wanted to know why the French had sent de Bienville to claim land that was clearly Iroquois territory. Warriors from Indian nations began to collect along the Ohio River.

The French decided it was time to show the British they meant business. They recruited a war party of Ojibwe and Ottawa to destroy a British trading post and the Miami Indian village next door, then started to build a chain of forts to block the British from access to the Ohio River.

The Shawnee and Lenape worried about the French taking over the area and appealed to the Iroquois Federation for help. Pennsylvania's intermediary, George Croghan, had by this time

A CENSUS OF THE NUMBER OF INDIAN WARRIORS IN THE OHIO VALLEY IN 1748

Cayuga	20	Oneida	15
Lenape (Delaware)	175	Onondaga	35
Huron	40	Seneca	163
Mohawk	74	Shawnee	162
Mohican	15	Wyandot	100
		Total:	**789**

married an Indian woman and taken on her people's ways so much that people were calling him "the White Mingo." Croghan used his influence to appeal to the Iroquois to stop the French. The Iroquois responded by giving Virginia permission to build a blockhouse on the Ohio River, and George Washington made a second trip to the area for the Ohio Land Company. Though his Indian guides suggested he build the fort on a high elevation, Washington instead chose the site of Diondega, the point where the rivers meet. He reported back, and Virginia sent 100 men to the area to build Fort Prince George.

While the Virginian soldiers were building their fort, two French traders and two French soldiers disguised themselves and infiltrated their ranks. They soon discovered that the captain and his lieutenant had gone, leaving an ensign in charge. The spies reported to their commander, and before the fort was completed the French had cannons aimed at Diondega. Seeing that the French force was five times their size, the Virginian ensign accepted the gracious terms of surrender offered by the French and marched his men back home.

The French demolished the fort and built their own in its place, naming it for their Canadian governor, the Marquis Duquesne. Meanwhile, Washington built another post less than 100 miles south. When his Virginia militia attacked an advance unit of 30 French, killed its commander and imprisoned the survivors, the tension that had been building between France and Britain became a full-fledged war.

In retaliation, Washington's 350 men were attacked by 700 French. Again the French were gracious, allowing the defeated troops to march back to Virginia with a promise that they would not build another fort on the Ohio for at least one full year.

By this time, part of the Ohio River had been given the name Allegheny, from the Indian word Allegewi meaning "fair water."

General Edward Braddock arrived in Virginia from England after Washington's defeat to lead an attack on Fort Duquesne. He invited Washington to join him and gave him the honorary title of colonel. They marched their troops, which numbered more than 2,000 and included 500 colonials and two Irish regiments, up Nemacolin's Path toward Fort Duquesne.

When the local Lenape and Shawnee chose to stay out of the fighting—no Lenape would join the French, and only four Shawnee—the French appealed to the Great Lakes and St. Lawrence tribes, where they were able to amass an army of 300 French Canadians and 600 Indians. Near the mouth of Turtle Creek, the French and Indian forces caught Braddock's army in an ambush.

Braddock, steeped in British military training, insisted that his soldiers fight the battle in rigid, exposed rows. When one Virginia soldier attempted to take cover and shoot at the enemy from behind a tree, Braddock called him a coward and ran him through with his sword. The soldier's brother, who was fighting beside him, shot Braddock. Braddock died on the battlefield and, by the end of the battle, half his men had also perished. George Washington, at 23 years old, was named commander of all Virginia troops.

Most white men at this time did not distinguish between Indian tribes—as far as they were concerned, Indians were Indians—so British colonists were outraged against all Indians after Braddock's defeat. When representatives of the Shawnee and Lenape traveled to Ohio to protest the Iroquois allowing the British to settle in the Ohio Valley, the British hanged them. The Lenape and Shawnee declared war.

Though settlement in the area had been forbidden by the British—a fact that especially angered the wealthy colonists who had money invested in the Ohio Land Company—a few folks had been quietly ignoring the edict, building cabins and starting farms. With warring factions all around them, they began to band together and build small forts near their homes in the hope that the extra protection would keep them safe from an Indian attack.

Back east, Mary and John Turner and the boys had moved from their cabin into the British fort near their home, and they weren't there long when Old Indian Town was attacked. A chief called Old Smoke led a war party that set the fort on fire and demanded immediate surrender. While those inside the fort were discussing their options, John Turner took it upon himself to choose for them and threw open the doors of the fort. Everyone inside was taken prisoner by the Indians.

The Indians captured them at Fort Granville, around Lewisburg. And they forced march to Kittanning.

The prisoners were marched at a furious pace, traveling an Indian trail along the Allegheny River to Kittanning. They covered 130 miles in three days, each prisoner loaded up with loot from the fort. Turner carried 100 pounds of salt. As Turner's luck would have it, Tewa, the chief of the Kittanning village, was the brother of Fish, the Indian that Turner and Girty had killed five years before. Turner was painted black to signify that he was to be put to death, and burned at the stake—in front of his family.

Prisoners were spoils of war in an Indian raid, but not all were killed or even mistreated. Many were adopted or, as the Indians called it, "brought into the tribe."

To prove themselves, most captives had to "run the gauntlet." In this rite, a goal was pointed out to the prisoner, perhaps a cabin or tree some distance away. Then the Indians would form two rows

Washington's post was built near what is now Confluence, Pennsylvania.

The sash that General Edward Braddock wore with his military uniform was used as a litter to carry him from the battlefield after he was shot. George Washington took the general's bloodstained sash and carried it with him every time he went into battle thereafter.

on either side of the captive, who was expected to run toward the goal while the Indians screamed and beat them with sticks. To the white man, this seemed a completely cruel and barbarous act; to the Indian, it was a test of worthiness. If prisoners made it to the goal, they had shown their bravery and strength and were often adopted into the tribe. (When Indians did this to other Indians, since they were familiar with the ritual, the captured Indians concentrated all their effort on running as fast as they could!) The degree of brutality of the gauntlet varied among Indian tribes. For some, it was fierce; for others, it consisted simply of a couple of light blows on the back.

Those captives chosen to be adopted underwent ceremonial rites. Some had their heads shaved except for a scalplock. Some were painted red. Other tribes had a ceremony that was much like a baptism, with prisoners dunked in the water to have their white blood washed away. No matter which adoption ritual was used, afterward there was no longer any distinction between adopted Indians and those born to the tribe.

> *If you had been captured as a young boy or a young girl by a Great Lakes tribe, especially Seneca, they would have pierced your nose to show that you had been indoctrinated into the tribe. They did this so that you would not be confused with a captive, but recognized as one that actually had been brought into the tribe. Once you were adopted into the tribe, you lived just like they did; there was no difference. You were treated good.*

Adoptees were taken in and raised by families. Boys and men were trained to become braves; women and girls helped to hoe corn and care for the home. From the day of their adoption, they had all tribal privileges, including the opportunity to become chief.

> *In Kittanning, that's where everyone was separated. James was taken by the Shawnee, Simon was taken by the Seneca, and John Jr., George and the mother were taken by the Lenape.*

Mary, George and young John were the first of the family to leave Kittanning. They were taken first to Fort Duquesne, where John Jr. was baptized by a French priest at the fort, then down the Ohio River to an Indian village named Logstown in what is now Beaver County.

James was taken by the Shawnee to Ohio. Old Smoke, the Seneca chief who led the raid, took Simon with him to New York's Finger Lakes area to raise him as his son. Ironically, the Girty boys began to find a stability with the Indians that they never knew at home.

> *Simon was captured at the age of 15 and stayed with them until he was about 23 or 24, which was a very impressionable age, and he*

found a greater love and closeness with them, which is why he adopted their clothing and style. They strongly influenced him.

Thomas remained in Kittanning, but not for long.

Thomas stayed at Kittanning for about a month, but a colonel named Armstrong who was with British militia outside Fort Pitt came and rescued him. So Thomas wasn't a captive long enough to be brought into the tribe.

After the Battle of Blanket Hill in Kittanning, Lieutenant Colonel John Armstrong was surprised to find that many of the white adoptees were not happy to see him. Most, in fact, refused his offer of liberation and stayed with their tribe.

Back in Virginia, the British were gearing up for another attempt to take Fort Duquesne. Brigadier General John Forbes, assisted by Commander George Washington and a Swiss mercenary named Henry Bouquet, took 5,000 colonial troops and 1,500 Scottish Highlanders up Nemacolin's Path to Pennsylvania. Near Raystown they began to cut a new path—a bit longer, but it would take them through areas where they would have access to fresh horses. All along the way, the soldiers built forts so the troops could fall back if necessary. Forbes supervised the work himself, taking care that the men in his command were friendly and generous with any Indians they encountered along the way.

As the army approached Fort Duquesne, General Forbes sent 800 men ahead with Major James Grant to quietly scout the area and capture prisoners to question back at the base. When they came within a mile of the fort, Grant decided instead to announce their presence with a drum and bagpipe chorus. His battalion was greeted by a well-prepared enemy. Three hundred of Grant's soldiers were killed. The victors created a gruesome tableau as a warning, hanging the heads of the Highlanders on posts, their tartans flying in the breeze beneath them.

Grant's surviving soldiers limped back and found Forbes and his men in Ligonier at one of the forts built during their march. The general marched the troops forward to a camp near the old battleground at Braddock's Field. They were planning their next move when a far-off explosion lit the sky. The French had learned their supply line from Canada was closed because of a snowstorm and decided to cut their losses, so they lit their ammunition stores and sent Fort Duquesne up in a fiery blast.

With the French retreating downriver, Forbes brought his men to the ruins at the Point and started making plans to build a much larger fort. Washington retired, at the ripe old age of 26, with the title of brigadier general. The Girty boys grew up in their adopted Indian families, and the Indians tried to negotiate treaties that would give them a measure of stability in what obviously was a rapidly changing land. When peace did come with the Treaty of Easton, it came at a high price: all adopted Indians had to be returned to their former homes. ♦

THE GIRTY BOYS

3

For the Indians to return the white members of their tribe to their "place of basic origin," meaning the British fort nearest where they had been captured, was not an easy task. There were *so*  many captives—some estimate as many as 700—and they were spread out among various tribes across hundreds of miles. For many Indian families, more difficult than the logistics were matters of the heart. Following this edict meant parting with their loved ones.

> *Simon did not want to leave New York state, nor did the natives want him to go. The chief that adopted him, Koyingwaurtos, looked at him as a son and was really saddened, and so was Simon.*

Many of the white captives were not the least bit interested in being surrendered to the British. But to uphold their end of the treaty, their tribes had to comply. Many an Indian father had to tie his wife's or child's hands and feet when he left them at the fort so they wouldn't come running after him. The farewell scenes were heart-breaking.

Various treaties were drawn up to support the Easton treaty and, as their chiefs signed them, one by one James, George, Simon and Mary Girty were delivered to Mercer's Fort, the temporary building General John Stanwix was using as a base of operations while he supervised construction of the new fort at the Point. This ambitious bastion would be the largest of the frontier forts, and his men were busy at work, using brick made from clay dug on Ayers Hill, wood cut at a mill on Saw Mill Run and stone quarried on nearby Herron Hill. Stanwix planned to name the fort in honor of the radical British statesman, William Pitt.

Colonel William Crawford, a good friend of General George Washington, took the Girtys into his home. Simon was soon fast friends with Crawford's son John and John's cousin, Van Swearingen. Seventeen-year-old Van Swearingen was fascinated with the Girty boys and their Indian ways, and at his request the boys

As many as half the white captives did eventually escape and return to their Indian families.

Duquesne University now stands on Ayers Hill.

Saw Mill Run flowed into the Ohio about a mile below the Point.

There was a moat entirely surrounding Fort Pitt, which made it inaccessible by land unless you went over a drawbridge. But the water was channeled from the Allegheny River, and there was a water entrance to the fort on the western side.

conspired to arrange a "kidnapping" by the Shawnee so he could become an Indian, too.

John's sister Sarah caught Simon's eye, but the Crawfords were the first "genteel" family in the West, and their daughter had higher aspirations than to take up with a white Indian. She married a rich young man from a prominent Virginia family.

The British did not consider the treaties they had signed as accords between two equal nations. As far as they were concerned, they were the conquering nation and the Indians the conquered. They treated the natives accordingly, and their first order of business was to stop trade of two items a conquering nation did not sell to its conquered: gunpowder and lead. They also banned the sale of rum to natives, fearing the Indians would get "out of control." The Indians were equally troubled by reports from their spies. The British were breeding English mastiffs—one-hundred-fifty-pound dogs that stood nearly three feet high—and training them to kill Indians. Sermons in British churches were preaching that to kill an Indian was almost a Christian duty. The Indians had good reason to believe that these Long Knives were planning to eradicate their tribes.

Pontiac, an Ottawa chief at Detroit, had recently been converted to a religion taught by a Lenape prophet named Neolin. Neolin urged a return to traditional Indian ways, which meant rejecting trade goods acquired through the white man, especially their rum. He asked his followers to forget tribal differences and unite against the white man. Neolin already had a large following among the Lenape who, along with the Shawnee and Seneca, had been talking about war. When these tribes sent emissaries to Detroit to see if the Ottawa wanted to help wage war on the British, Pontiac's answer was an emphatic yes.

After about a year of planning, nearly every Indian nation in the Old Northwest had banded together with Pontiac for an attack on the British forces. They began with raids on the settlements, and most settlers fled to whatever fort was nearby or simply moved back east. While the Long Knives were on edge because of the raids, the Indian tribes launched a simultaneous attack of all British forts west of the Appalachians.

When this blitz hit Fort Pitt, its commander, Captain Simon Ecuyer, took every action he could think of. He burned the houses in the village that sat above the Point on Grant's Hill, the old battleground where the Highlanders had died. He tore down homes along the rivers and ordered all settlers into the fort where he could protect them. He drafted every able-bodied man into his militia. He built blockhouses to defend the moat around Fort Pitt when Indians started creeping along the channel and shooting flaming arrows through the fort's gunwales.

A Lenape warrior named Turtle Heart approached Fort Pitt with the news that Indian troops were on their way and it would be best if the British evacuated. Ecuyer remembered a letter he had received from General Jeffrey Amherst. The letter contained a suggestion, made by Henry Bouquet, to employ a diabolical tactic. Following its instructions, Ecuyer sent the Delaware a deadly gift in reply to their warning—a box of blankets that had been used by smallpox victims. This strategy, perhaps the first case of biological warfare, created an epidemic that spread not only through the Indian tribes but also through British colonies across the southeast, eventually killing thousands of people.

The fort, by this time, had been cut off from provisions for quite a while. Ecuyer and his people needed food. Bouquet, who was now a colonel, was assigned to bring it, and he led 460 men and 340 packhorses loaded with sacks of flour toward the Point. After two weeks of hard marching, they were about to make camp at Bushy Run when Indians attacked. Bouquet's men were able to protect

One of the blockhouses built by Captain Ecuyer's men is still standing today.

Bushy Run is near Harrison City, Pennsylvania.

THE RUNS AND THEIR LOCATIONS

Three Mile Run, left bank
  Brady Street in South Oakland
Three Mile Run, right bank
  Bates Street in South Oakland
Four Mile Run, right bank
  near Greenfield Avenue in Greenfield
Six Mile Run (Street's Run)
  at the base of the Glenwood Bridge in Hays
Nine Mile Run
  opposite Homestead on the border of Squirrel Hill

themselves by stacking the flour bags and using them as a makeshift fort. The Indians were forced to retreat, and the conflict became one of the very few Western battles that the white men won. Bouquet and his men reached Fort Pitt four days later and ended the siege. By then, Indians had captured every British bastion in the West except for three: Fort Niagara, Fort Detroit and Fort Pitt.

A peace treaty was signed at the fork of the Muskingum River in Black Bear Town. The treaty stated that Indians were welcome to come to the fort to trade but they could no longer live in the land between the rivers. By this time, it was obvious to the Delaware and Shawnee that the British had splintered into Pennsylvanians and Virginians and would continue fighting over the land at the Point. They had seen this kind of thing before and were relieved to get out of the line of fire. Most of them moved west to Ohio. True to the Indians' predictions, the Penn family of Pennsylvania and the Calvert family of Maryland hired two British surveyors to define

The northern path from the Girty farm led out Shady Avenue through Squirrel Hill to Forbes Avenue.

The Girty claim went west as far as the current site of Beehner Road, east to where Shady Avenue now sits, and north in an irregular pattern across the valley that is now Beechwood Boulevard as far as Covode Street.

the borders of Pennsylvania, Maryland and Virginia. Charles Mason and Jeremiah Dixon got started on the daunting task.

The British still had a large military force at Fort Pitt, which meant they needed plenty of food for the men and corn for the horses. The Girty boys, now reunited except for their youngest brother John, decided to move to the country to join the ranks of farmers who supplied these items. They headed up the Monongahela to the dense forest above Four Mile Run, where they found the perfect location for their farm. There was fertile land, and lots of game in case times got lean. They could take produce downriver on the Monongahela or to the Point by land—there was a path that led north to follow Forbes Trail and another down Four Mile Run to Braddock's Field Path, which followed the river to Grant's Hill.

At the top of a hill between Four Mile Run and Six Mile Run, the boys notched trees with a hatchet to claim their "tomahawk rights" to the land. Starting at a spring filled with cool, clear water at the top of Brown's Hill near the salt lick, they marked their border, cleared the land and started to farm.

True to their Indian ways, Mary Girty tended the fields while her sons traveled. Because they spoke so many Indian languages, it was easy for them to find work as interpreters and traders. All the boys kept in close contact with the tribes that raised them and constantly asked if anyone had seen their youngest brother John, who never had been surrendered to the British.

Except for their white skin, it was difficult to tell the Girty boys from the Indians. They became known across the West for their skill as interpreters—and for their wild ways.

They say Simon would out-Indian the Indians. If the Indians rode a horse backwards, he rode a horse standing on his head. If the Indians traveled 100 miles, he traveled 150 miles. That's the kind of guy he was, that's how he got their respect. He once went 92 miles in 48 hours in a snowstorm to warn an Indian village that white soldiers were coming to attack them. On foot, in the dead of winter. So he was a pretty tough guy.

John Turner Jr. was already a young man when his brothers finally located him in a tribe in Canada. Their little brother had grown up tall and thin with long black hair and snapping dark eyes. At first, John spoke plenty of Indian dialects but hardly any English, but that was remedied when he went with his brothers to their mother and settled down at her cabin near the spring. Thomas, his wife Ann and their two children, John and Nancy, lived on one side of them, and George lived on the other.

Their cabins, though sturdy, were not much different from the huts they had shared with the Indians. Logs were notched at the end and locked together to build the frame. More logs were

split to make the roof. The spaces between logs were filled with the clay that could be found everywhere near their cabins. If there was any light in the house, it came through the door or through a window covered with paper smeared with bear's grease to give it a little transparency.

The family slept on the dirt floor of their cabin and had their meals at a homemade table. They cut and ate their dinner with a knife—forks were only used by the genteel, which the Girtys certainly were not. But the food they ate was fit for a king. There were plenty of fish in the rivers, where catfish grew to weigh a hundred pounds. Hunting was great near the salt lick, and they dined on bear, squirrel, venison and partridges.

The squirrels were becoming quite a nuisance, eating seed planted in the fields and grain stored for winter, and running across the cabin roofs keeping everyone awake at night. The area began to be known by the name of Squirrel Hill, and the shortcut from Nemacolin's Path that ran along the ridge above the river became Squirrel Hill Road. With more and more travelers coming by, the dirt road was a little wider and more defined than it had been in years past. Salt Lick Trail was still a quiet lane through a forest of willow, elm and oak trees that grew so thick you couldn't see more than twenty feet in any direction. A walk down Salt Lick Trail took you from the salt lick at Brown's Hill north and then west through the forest to Braddock's Field Road along the Monongahela River. It passed a settlement at the bottom of the hill that had been started by some of the Scots from the village at the Point who were farming land between Four Mile Run and Six Mile Run. Their village was known as Scotch Bottom.

The Girty/Turner log cabin was in the area now bordered by Lilac, Windsor and Welfer streets and Beechwood Boulevard.

After being forced by the treaty to move further west, the Indians were appalled one day to find surveyors hired by George Washington for the Ohio Land Company in the heart of Shawnee country. The Shawnee sent them packing and told them to carry the message that any more surveyors found on their land would not live to talk about it. The surveyors soon returned and, as promised, the Indians attacked. A Long Knife named Michael Cresap, the Virginian who had helped blaze Nemacolin's Path, heard of the skirmish and in retaliation led a vigilante raid against a Shawnee trading party in Wheeling, killing their chief. A month later, another raid by Long Knives resulted in the massacre of peaceful Seneca, including the wife, brother and pregnant sister of Logan, the Seneca chief.

It looked like war again, and the Girty boys, always ready for a good fight, were eager to join in the fray. ♦

4 | Who's Fighting Who?

The threat of being scalped was enough to halt Mason and Dixon for a while. The two surveyors had drawn a boundary line that almost reached to the Point—when they quit, they were only ten miles away—but beyond that line there was no way of deciding who owned what. No one was surprised when Pennsylvania and Virginia each decided that the Ohio River Valley belonged to them. Pennsylvania opened a land office and began to sell land. Settlers, including the Girtys, filed claims for the land on which they were living. Soon Virginia opened its own land office, selling the same land at one-tenth of the price. Both Pennsylvania and Virginia set up their own systems of government and their own courts. Disputes were predictably hard to settle.

The village now called Pittsburgh was growing by leaps and bounds. One year, there were 88 men (not counting the soldiers, who included two companies of the Royal Irish), 29 women and 32 children, and the very next year, there were 324 men, 92 women and 41 children. Houses were built at the Point, along Water Street near the Monongahela River, and on Grant's Hill. Most of the villagers were from England, Ireland, Scotland and Germany, and new traders and Indian fighters appeared every day. They were a motley crew. Some were runaway indentured servants who came west to start a new life. Others were loyalists, people loyal to England's king, who opposed the War for Independence that had already started back east. Some were simply folks looking for adventure.

Inside the fort at the Point was the brick governor's mansion, and beyond it were orchards and vegetable gardens. But the villagers themselves lived in log houses and huts, making their own clothing from fabric they had spun on their spinning wheels, wearing moccasins cut from hides of animals they had eaten at long-forgotten suppers.

A thriving village needs a strong economy. Though Indians were no longer allowed to live in Pittsburgh, they were welcomed again with open arms at the trading posts to exchange their fur pelts for ammunition, blankets, rum and other goods. A typical trade list showed that 88 summer deerskins, six beaver, three fox, 13 raccoon, one bear and two wildcat hides were swapped for a supply of ammunition, knives, calico skirts, leggings, blankets, razors, coats and a tin kettle. Boatbuilding also became a busy industry in

INDENTURED SERVANT? WHAT DOES THAT MEAN?

An indentured servant was a type of temporary slave. Some people became indentured voluntarily, as apprentices to learn a craft. But most were criminals shipped to the colonies to serve out their jail term, thus relieving western Europe's overcrowded prisons.

It is estimated that as many as half the white settlers in North America were indentured servants. They were sometimes treated better, sometimes worse, than slaves, dependent entirely upon the kindness of their owner: a slave was a commodity whose value would drop if mistreated, but an indentured servant was a short-term purchase and thus had less resale value.

Pittsburgh, providing canoes for traders and travelers and flatboats to transport men and goods for the military.

With all the new settlers, it looked like Pittsburgh's economy was going to be based on farming now rather than trading. But roads were still no more than widened Indian trails through rough terrain, and refrigeration was not even yet a dream. How would farmers transport their produce over long distances? The answer was simple—whiskey. Whiskey didn't spoil or become bug-infested, and it was already as common on a Pennsylvanian's supper table as meat or bread. Pittsburgh became known far and wide for its fruit brandies, ciders and what some said was the best corn and rye whiskey made.

After the British abandoned Fort Pitt, Virginia's Lord Dunmore rode through the Ohio River Valley. He decided that Virginia could easily establish sole ownership of the area and sent Brigadier General Edward Hand to take command of the fort. Hand arrived and spread the word among the local men that he was looking for recruits. When word reached Squirrel Hill, Simon Girty and his younger brother John Turner went to the newly named Fort Dunmore and signed up along with 200 other local soldiers. Simon was given command of a troop sent to patrol the rivers and roads, confiscating any trade goods that were being traded by Pennsylvanians in what they claimed was the colony of Virginia. In short, they were employed as pirates.

Before long, Lord Dunmore got word that Virginia's Ohio Land Company wanted more land than simply the Ohio Valley. That meant heading west, which meant fighting the Shawnee and Mingo. Dunmore called his men home to prepare for battle.

The original plan was for Dunmore himself to lead 3,000 men down the Ohio River to Point Pleasant. There they would meet with an army of 1,500 led by Andrew Lewis, and together they would cross the Ohio toward the Shawnee villages along the Scioto River. But Dunmore, afraid of an ambush, changed his

mind at the last minute and took his men west instead, leaving Lewis stranded at his encampment. Cornstalk, the leader of the Shawnee, had already banded together with the Lenape, Mingo and Wyandot. He spotted Lewis and sent Pucksinwah, their war chief, with 500 warriors to the north bank of the Ohio River, across from Point Pleasant, to set up camp and plan an attack.

That day was a busy one for Lewis. First, a messenger showed up with a letter from Dunmore about his change of plan. Then two of his scouts accidentally stumbled into the Shawnee camp across the river. One managed to escape and report back to his commander, and Lewis, an experienced Indian fighter, knew he had to think quickly. He divided his men into three smaller forces. While the first two troops attacked the Indian camp from left and right, the third regiment cut logs to block the river path straight ahead. As Lewis hoped, Cornstalk led his men to the river path and, unable to break through, they were forced to retreat. Pucksinwah was killed in the battle and a younger warrior, a white adoptee who had grown up with the name Van Swearingen but was now known as Blue Jacket, was made war chief of the Shawnee nation.

The land-grabbing conflict between Virginia and Pennsylvania was put aside for the greater cause of American independence. General Hand heard there was an Indian village on the Cuyahoga River where the British had abandoned lots of ammunition and supplies. He called his troops back for a raid. In a deep, cold winter, Hand marched 500 soldiers into the Ohio country, but the weather forced them to turn back before they reached their destination. On their way home, his troops invaded another, peaceful Indian village. All

the men had gone hunting, and the women and children were alone and undefended. Hand's men attacked, and the Girty boys were appalled. If this "Squaw Campaign" was the way the American army operated, they wanted no part of it. They deserted.

> There were two reasons Simon Girty fought for the British. First off, he didn't like the way the Americans were treating the Indians. He went with Dunmore's troops to raid this Indian village and all the braves were gone, so they shot and killed some squaws and kids. He didn't think that was right. And second, he considered himself a loyalist. He was loyal to the king.

The American revolutionaries, who called themselves Patriots, issued a reward for Simon's capture. He and George signed their land over to their brother John Turner and left town.

> Simon left Pittsburgh along with McKee, who McKees Rocks is named after, and Matthew Elliott and a couple of Black guys, and he went to Detroit. There was a British fort there and they hired him as an interpreter.

John Turner ended up with 154 acres from his brothers and wisely named the property Federal Hill after the Patriot cause. He moved back to the farm and married a young woman named Susanna Clark, whose family came to Scotch Bottom from Baltimore. He built a new log cabin with four rooms, two up and two down, for his new bride. With John's mother, they continued farming and bringing produce to market at Pittsburgh.

The Indian trails, including Squirrel Hill Road, were widened now that wagons joined the horseback and walking traffic. It made for a pleasant journey, unlike Braddock's Field Road, which ran along the Monongahela River from the Point to Braddock's Field. New travelers along that road were shocked to see that the British had never buried their dead on the North Braddock battlefield. Hundreds of bones and skulls lay strewn on the ground, the putrefied remains covered with teeth marks where they had been chewed by wolves.

From the beginning of the War for Independence, the Indians were allied with Britain. Skirmishes between Indians and Patriots continued—with plenty of encouragement from the British, who had torn down Fort Pitt and sold its materials so that the villagers couldn't use the fort for protection. One of their governors, Henry Hamilton, had the Indian nickname of "Hair-buyer" because of the high price he was willing to pay for an American scalp.

Settlers in and around Pittsburgh worked hard to protect themselves and, during an Indian raid, might spend a week or more in one of the little "settler's forts" scattered throughout the country-side. John Turner and his family never needed to bother with the

Alexander McKee was a trader and had been George Croghan's assistant. A half-breed Indian and a loyalist, McKee gave the land he owned along Chartiers Creek, which included McKees Rocks, to his brother James.

John and Susanna Turner's cabin was on a hill near the corner where Frank Street meets Loretta Street.

fort in Squirrel Hill. John had quite a reputation for his skill with a rifle and, anyhow, his brother Simon might be the one leading the raids.

The Indians had so much respect for Simon Girty that he led war parties. He raided with the Indians a lot down through Pittsburgh. He stopped in to see his mother and his brother.

Lenape chief Hopocan, also known as Captain Pipe, was persuaded to join two other Lenape chiefs, White Eyes and Killbuck, to sign a treaty with the Patriots at Fort Pitt, the first treaty ever between Native Americans and those who hoped to form the new United States. The terms of the treaty were simple—the Patriots offered protection from the British and a Lenape representative in their Congress and, in exchange, the Patriots would be permitted to build a fort on Lenape land.

The treaty was broken by the Patriots almost as soon as it was signed. White Eyes declined an offer to join the Patriots' fight against the British, saying he preferred to live in peace. He was persuaded instead to act as a scout to lead Fort Pitt's new commander, General Lachlan McIntosh, to the site where the Patriots could build their new fort. McIntosh's men killed White Eyes and sent back a report that he had died of smallpox. Word reached the other tribes, and they began to band together to plan their next move.

In retaliation against the Indian raids, Captain David Williamson led his militia on a hunt to destroy an Indian village—any Indian village. When they happened upon Gnadenhutten, one of the Moravian mission villages of peaceful Christian Indians, Williamson's frontier militia took a vote as democratic citizens on what they should do next. They decided to kill the Indians. They gave them overnight to pray, and the next day killed 29 men, 27 women and 34 children in cold blood: they dragged them into a building, beat them to death with mallets, then took their scalps as evidence of the slaughter. Two Indian boys who had been scalped somehow survived, escaped to another Indian camp and reported what had happened. Captain Pipe, the Lenape war chief, learned that his mother and brother were killed in the massacre.

Moravian Lenapes were tied about the hands and ankles; women and children were put in one building and men in the other. The helpless Indians were in prayer when the militia tomahawked them and hacked the Indians to death.

Colonel William Crawford, who had befriended the Girtys at Fort Pitt, was leading an army of 450 men in the same general direction as Gnadenhutten in another attempt to retaliate against the Indian raids. Unfortunately for Crawford, he and his men encountered the Wyandot, who were furious with the Patriots and sympathetic with Captain Pipe. Crawford's soldiers fought for nearly 24 hours before they began to realize they could not prevail. The Indians were too full of anger to even let them retreat, and they ran through Crawford's troops as they scattered, scalping anyone they could catch. Colonel Crawford, his chaplain Dr. Knight and nine others were captured and taken prisoner. The Wyandot turned them over to Captain Pipe.

The prisoners were taken to the Indian camp, where Captain Pipe painted them black with wood ash paint, a designation that they were marked for execution. Simon Girty, Matthew Elliott and Alexander McKee were among Captain Pipe's men, and they began to ask the chief to spare Crawford's life, both because he had been good to the Girtys and because, being savvy in political dealings, they knew that burning a friend of the Patriots' commander-in-chief, George Washington, would not be taken lightly.

When they were going to burn Crawford, Simon tried three times to get him loose. He even offered them his prize white horse; he had silver mounted pistols, he offered them. Three times he tried, and finally they said, "You better shut up, or we're gonna burn you, too."

Their pleas were to no avail. Captain Pipe would have revenge on the people who killed his mother and his brother. Crawford was tortured and finally put to death. Dr. Knight escaped and brought the story back to civilization.

The next year, a treaty was signed in Paris giving the newly born United States of America all territory between the Ohio River and the Great Lakes. But news traveled slowly, and it had not yet reached the Ohio Valley and the Turner farm beyond.

Over the hill from Greenfield down in what they used to call Burkhart's Glen, Simon was on a spying mission for the Indians and captured a kid named Burkhart who was out with his cows. Simon asked him, "What's the bells ringing at Fort Pitt for?" The kid told him, "The war's over"—you know, the American Revolution. Simon didn't believe him, so he took him to Canada as a prisoner. When he got there he found out the war was over, and he brought him back to Greenfield. 'Course, Simon brought the kid back and turned him loose and beat it, since he had a price on his head.

The War for Independence was over, but not the war between the Indians and the Patriots. The Indians knew now that the Americans' treaties were not worth the breath with which they were spoken. Settlers still took refuge in forts along the countryside, and the British continued to supply the Indians with weapons.

Over a decade passed before the British decided to turn their back on their Indian allies in favor of a treaty with the Americans. The decision was made only after Blue Jacket, their best strategist

Burkhart's Glen was on Brown's Hill, which reached from the Monongahela River to Squirrel Hill Road.

Pittsburgh's first
fire company,
The Eagle, was
formed the same
year that John
Neville's house
burned down.

*Pittsburgh's first
fire company,
The Eagle, was
formed the same
year that John
Neville's house
burned down.*

*The average
keelboat was
sixty feet long and
ten feet wide, with
a large cabin in the
center of the deck.
A flatboat was
more like a large
raft, and could
carry a house,
cattle, a wagon
and even a garden,
almost like a
floating farm.*

and now war chief for the entire Indian alliance, was compelled to order his warriors to retreat from a battle at Fallen Timbers. It was painfully obvious to everyone that the Indians would be forced once again to move west.

A peace treaty was signed at Greenville. Miami Chief Little Turtle, as a representative of the Indian alliance, agreed to give the land in Ohio and parts of Michigan, Indiana and Illinois to the Americans. In return, each tribe would receive annual payments of trade goods. Certain chiefs, including Little Turtle and Blue Jacket, were secretly given yearly salaries to make sure the treaties were upheld by their people.

When it came time for the chiefs to sign the pact, one young chief named Tecumseh, the son of fallen Shawnee war chief Pucksin-wah, refused. Instead he gave a stirring speech, declaring that the land was like air and water and belonged to everyone. The Indians were impressed with Tecumseh's oratory skills and made him their representative in future councils. Even the Americans compared him to their own Henry Clay.

The peace treaty signed at Greenville lasted more than a decade, until Tecumseh's brother Tenksatawa revived Neolin's religion and helped to unite the tribes again against the Long Knives in battles much further west.

By now, distilling had become the most profitable business in Pittsburgh, and more whiskey, brandy and cider were made there than anywhere else in the country. More than one-fifth of Pittsburgh's farmers were also distillers. Before the United States of America was twenty years old, its Congress passed a liquor tax to raise money toward the national debt. This may have gone over well in the larger eastern cities, but in the Ohio Valley where whiskey was king, revenuers who came to collect the tariff ran the risk of being escorted out of town at the end of a shotgun.

By the third year of this tax, Pittsburghers had had enough. Five hundred farmers stormed the home of the local tax inspector, John Neville, and burned it to the ground. George Washington, now president of the new United States, received intelligence reports that the vigilantes were holding a meeting at Braddock's Field to plan their next move. He decided that his new country needed to make a show of strength and sent in an overwhelming militia of 13,000 soldiers scraped together from four surrounding states. Outnumbered 26 to one, the rebels wisely cut their losses and went home. A few were arrested but later pardoned.

Though it may seem so, Pittsburgh's economy didn't rely just on whiskey. There was a new, lucrative line of trade: travelers. The freshly printed American Universal Geography called the Ohio River "the most beautiful river on earth." More importantly, because it was so difficult to cross the Appalachian Mountains, the Ohio River was the logical entrance to the West. Folks who were westward bound abandoned their wagons in Pittsburgh to buy a boat for the next leg of their trip. Some of the boat builders who had military contracts stayed on after the army left and now catered to these travelers, providing keelboats and flatboats to take them west to the Missouri River or south as far as New Orleans, and even into the ocean beyond.

Charles Mason and Jeremiah Dixon finally finished their survey and the Mason-Dixon Line was drawn. Boundary disputes between Virginia and Pennsylvania were settled, and Pennsylvania won the Ohio Valley and the rough-and-ready town within. Pittsburgh, Pennsylvania, full of seasoned settlers and Indian fighters, got ready to take advantage of the travelers who seemed to multiply overnight like rabbits. Inns and taverns were built, providing work not only for innkeepers but also for farmers and distillers. Some of these westward-bound folks saw the opportunities in Pittsburgh and decided to stay. Stores and factories began to emerge in the quickly growing town. ♦

5 | City Folks and Country Folks

*John George
Woods' stone
house, built on
what is now
the corner of
Chatsworth and
Tullymet streets in
Hazelwood, is still
standing.*

*Irvine Street
was named after
William Irvine,
the general in
charge of Fort Pitt
during the
Indian uprising.*

As Pittsburgh grew, so did the small towns around it. Years before, Colonel George Woods surveyed Pittsburgh for the Penns and was paid for his efforts with the land in Scotch Bottom. Now his grandson, John George Woods, owned more than a thousand acres in the fertile river valley. Though no one in the Woods family had ever used the land, when John George Woods married, he decided to live there with his bride and built a two-story stone house down past the stretch of road the Scotch Bottom settlers were calling Irvine Street. The Woods farm stretched between Four Mile Run and Six Mile Run and a mile back, up through the forest on the hillside, with one corner bordering the Turner farm. The house, surrounded by orchards and flower gardens, was quite a contrast to the log homes of the squatters along the river. There was plenty of talk in Scotch Bottom about the rich fellow moving in and how things might change. Folks doubted it would be for the better.

Up over the hill, John Turner's town was still overrun with squirrels—Turner joked about it, bragging that he could stand in his cabin doorway and shoot enough squirrels for supper. But otherwise, life had changed dramatically for Turner and his family. The British gave his brother Simon a pension that included a hundred acre farm in Canada, across the river from Detroit. Simon Girty lived there now with his wife, White Pigeon, an adoptee born with the name of Catherine Malott who had been raised by the Shawnee. Thomas and his family moved away and opened a trading post on the Allegheny River in a town called Girty's Run. James went west and now had a trading post in Girty's Town. George was off with the Indians, no one was sure exactly where. Mary Girty passed away, and John laid his mother to rest next to the two Indians he shot for trying to steal his ax.

Now an old woman called Granny McElroy lived in the old Girty cabin next to the spring, and there were more and more folks living nearby. Old Jake Castleman had the next farm down toward the river. The Sutch family was up on the knob of the hill. William Stewart, who everybody just called Killymoon, was busy building an inn near the salt lick where he planned to serve his homemade whiskey to travelers who took the shortcut up Brown's Hill.

Nowadays Squirrel Hill looked more like farmland than forest. John and Susanna Turner's farm was a lucrative business. They didn't have children of their own, but Susanna's sisters lived nearby

Killymoon's inn stood at the present location of Beechwood Gardens.

The wealthy built homes east of the city in what would become Point Breeze, Shadyside and Squirrel Hill. At the time, you could still get lost in the forest where Highland Avenue now stands.

and they were very close to their nieces and nephews, especially the three who were named after them—Susanna Halstead, Turner Blashford and John McCaslin.

Wherever he went, John Turner carried his rifle, and everyone knew John was the best shot in town. He started to hold turkey shoots for the neighbor men, and the hunting parties evolved into a "cork and gun" club called the Turner Rifles. After they passed the rigorous tryout—they say a Turner Rifle could hit a turkey's left eye at a hundred yards—the men had a built-in excuse for rowdy hunting excursions, taking off with a rifle in one hand and a bottle of whiskey in the other.

Traveling preachers held camp meetings near Turner's farm in an attempt to quell "these heathen men." They had their work cut out for them. Many times the meeting's tent ropes would be cut before the preaching even began, and even well-intentioned men attending the meeting would occasionally rise during the service to fight a man they accused of being too disruptive.

As the village of Pittsburgh transformed into a small city, it also became noisy and congested. Some of the wealthy people began to look for land in the surrounding country to build summer homes where they could get away from the heat and grime. East of the city was beautiful woodland, much of it unsettled. The air was fresh and crisp, the hunting spectacular, all in all a perfect place for a prosperous man to build a country house.

It came as no surprise that these outsiders did not mix well with the pioneers near Turner's farm. The newcomers, some of whom

After Hugh Henry Brackenridge, who regularly wrote editorials for John Scull's Gazette (precursor of today's Pittsburgh Post-Gazette), had a heated and well-publicized quarrel with Scull, Brackenridge started his own rival newspaper, Tree of Liberty.

The myth of Simon Girty as a villain has grown and lingered even until today.

were educated and considered themselves "civilized," looked down their noses at the country folk and called them Simple Simons. Turner and his neighbors called the city folk Dusters, saying they couldn't tell a turkey from a feather duster.

The stories that Hugh Henry Brackenridge was spreading about John Turner's brother Simon Girty didn't help matters any. Brackenridge, who moved to Pittsburgh from Philadelphia, was an Indian hater from way back. He considered all Indians animals, no matter how cosmopolitan or refined—even men like John Montour, an educated captain who led a company of Lenape for the Continental Army. But Brackenridge equally despised white frontier people who didn't live in the "civilized" way that he and other Philadelphians did. Though plenty of people knew Simon Girty's true story, Brackenridge had control of a newspaper and books in which to publish his version of Simon's escapades, which he hoped would put people on the right track.

Of course, Simon *had* supported the king during the Revolution. Everyone knew that—so had lots of local settlers, though they were smart enough to keep quiet and sit on the right side of the fence when the war was over. But Simon had also been a successful and famous Indian warrior—just the type of man local boys were apt to emulate. Brackenridge made it his personal mission to make sure that the boys would hate Girty and instead admire educated, civilized white people like himself. He wrote an account of Captain Pipe's execution of Colonel Crawford that made Girty more of a villain than Captain Pipe. Published in Philadelphia, away from conflicting reports in the British Army records farther west, he

developed a wide readership, and those back east perpetuated his myth of Simon as a villain.

Brackenridge's stories didn't have the desired effect on the settlers' sons, who were, every one, hoping to be a Turner Rifle when they were old enough, and any settler's daughter who hoped to marry up in station by dating a Duster put her rich young man in jeopardy of being beaten up by a gang of farm boys on his way home from her house.

Settlers' boys congregated on hills and in hollows to practice their shooting. The most common target that wasn't alive was an "Indian head," a piece of dough about the size of an acorn. They flattened it against a tree, paced off ten yards, turned and shot. If they could draw feathers around the marker with their rifle balls to resemble an Indian head, they were ready for a tryout with the Turner Rifles.

Susanna Turner, who had grown up in Baltimore, was a Christian woman, and at her request John Turner got together with some local men to build a little log church on Turner's land. The town didn't have a preacher, so settlers took turns conducting services themselves. The church roof was constantly full of holes because the local boys, always practicing their marksmanship, got into the habit of shooting squirrels off the roof. If folks went to church on a rainy day, they made sure to go early to find a dry place to sit.

The Iroquois "half-king" Guyasuta lived in what is now Sharpsburg.

The population in Pittsburgh grew to a whopping 1,565 people. The population of the new country itself was more than five million—four million white settlers and one million slaves—but almost all of them lived east of the Appalachian mountains. There were free Blacks in Pittsburgh: Charles Richards owned Black Charley's Inn near the center of town, and among the new settlers were a few Black soldiers, doctors and riverboat captains. There were very few slaves in the city, simply because the townspeople couldn't afford them. Most slaves in the area worked on plantations outside the city near Turtle Creek or farther out in Fayette County, where the largest plantation had twenty-four slaves and seven free Blacks. Though there was a law that Blacks born after March 1, 1780, would be free when they reached the age of 28, anyone born before that date remained a slave for life. A law passed eight years later, however, did free any slave brought to Pittsburgh by a new settler.

Most new Pittsburghers were from the British Isles, though there were some Germans, some French and a few Italians. The Indians were long gone, and even Guyasuta had moved to join the Seneca living along the Niagara River. But other than the streets near the Point and the village on Grant's Hill, Pittsburgh was still mostly countryside. There were two large ponds—actually three, if you counted the moat from the fort, which was usually full of wild ducks.

Methodism was becoming popular in England, and Europe was becoming orderly, mannerly and…well, stuffy. Pittsburgh was about as far from that description as you could get. Except for Market Street, which was paved, its roads were more mud than dirt. Animals, wild and domestic, ran through the streets day and night. Once or twice a year, Pennsylvania sent a judge to the Ohio River Valley, but otherwise the citizens were pretty much left to their own devices.

Actual crimes were not much of a problem. Once in a while there was a hanging, but people still slept with their doors open—though that might have been because few owned anything worth stealing. "Wickedness," however, abounded. Drinking was rampant, and even the most respectable residents were occasionally found on the side of the road sleeping it off. The noise of the animals at night was often broken up by gunshots as drunks rowdily galloped through town. Pittsburgh did have an ordinance against this, but no one paid attention to it.

Even prominent citizens broke the law. A feud between a local politician and a newspaper editor started with critical letters to the editor, grew to include accusations of the politician having a "colored" mistress, and culminated in a duel—quite against the law—on the banks of the Monongahela at the foot of Three Mile

Run. Tarleton Bates, the politician, died after the second shot and was buried along Virgin Alley in Trinity Churchyard. The man who shot him (curiously, not the editor but a young shopkeeper) got away with it—he took off for Baltimore and no one ever saw him again.

An interesting dichotomy is the fact that, during this time, Pittsburghers were also subject to "blue laws." Named for the color of the paper they were written on, the government of Pennsylvania created blue laws to ensure that no work would be done and no fun would be had on the Sabbath, a day that should be instead reserved for quiet reflection.

The new country's borders now reached west as far as the Mississippi River, and there were few ways to travel west without passing through Pittsburgh. Squirrel Hill Road saw more and more traffic, and Viewland, Killymoon's inn at the top of Brown's Hill, was full of cattlemen and stagecoach drivers pounding down his three-cents-a-shot whiskey.

The 320 miles between Philadelphia and Pittsburgh was now a mere 13-day trip. Every dozen miles or so, all the way from Philadelphia to Pittsburgh, a long wooden pike blocked passage until a toll was paid, at which time the pole would be turned to the side of the road so the traveler could pass. The part of the road between Lancaster and Philadelphia was already paved with limestone and gravel, and there was talk about using stones to pave the local leg of the trip along Penn Avenue. Though folks still walked the road, stagecoaches carrying mail and passengers were a common sight.

The flatboats and keelboats that left Pittsburgh couldn't return upstream, so westward-bound travelers needed a never-ending supply of new boats. Boatbuilding was a big business. When President Thomas Jefferson sent Meriwether Lewis to explore the west with William Clark, Lewis came to Pittsburgh to get boats for the expedition. While in Pittsburgh, Lewis hired two young men to join his trip, but all three were in Pittsburgh much longer than expected since the crafts had to be constructed between the boatbuilder's drinking binges.

Other industries were developing. Isaac Craig and James O'Hara started up a glassworks on Coal Hill along the Monongahela River. Sam Haslam opened a cotton factory. Coal was so plentiful it was used on the boats for ballast. Iron ore had been discovered, and there were nail factories opening up. And George Anshutz, Anthony Beelen and William Amberson got together and opened what looked like it might be a lucrative business: an iron furnace. ◆

TRAVEL AND TROUBLES

6

You can talk all you like about liberty and religious freedom, but when it comes right down to it, Western Pennsylvania was settled because of one simple, driving force—money. First there were the French traders, then Virginia's Ohio Land Company came looking to expand its operations. Now there was money to be made serving travelers headed for the Mississippi Valley.

With the Appalachian Mountains blocking travel from back east, the most feasible route to the western territory was still either by river or on the turnpike, both of which took you through Western Pennsylvania. Plenty of people were using a shortcut from the Monongahela River, traveling Squirrel Hill Road or Salt Lick Road on their way to Pittsburgh or nearby Hazelwood where they could buy boats and provisions to take them to their chosen area of the western frontier. Travelers often complained that they were being taken advantage of, overcharged or just plain cheated. But it was no use to argue: if you wanted to travel west, this was the only game in town.

There was an inn at the corner of Gladstone and Alma streets, and another at the corner of Kearcher Street and Greenfield Avenue. The second is still standing.

Killymoon wasn't the only one capitalizing on the travelers passing over Squirrel Hill Road. There was another inn farther on along the ridge, and yet another coming down the hill. Along the road between the two, a blacksmith shoed horses and mended wagon wheels.

Nearly everyone complained about the streets in the Ohio River territory— they were narrow and lopsided and crossed each other at odd angles—but at least the means of travel improved. Conestoga wagons could replace a whole team of packhorses with just a few horses, a wagon and a driver. With a system of relays to get new horses and drivers, two tons of goods could travel from Philadelphia to Pittsburgh in only six days. Wagons from Baltimore and Philadelphia covered the 350 miles to the Point over the Allegheny mountains in record time.

The Hazelwood
docs were located
at the bottom of
Hazelwood
Avenue along
the Monongahela
River.

WHY DO AMERICANS DRIVE ON THE LEFT SIDE OF THE CAR, AND TRAVEL ON THE RIGHT SIDE OF THE ROAD?

This custom began with the design of the popular covered wagons first built in Conestoga, Pennsylvania (near Lancaster) at the turn of the 19th century. The brake was on the left side of the wagon, so the driver would walk near the brake or ride on the lazyboard above it. Since the driver was on the left, for visibility's sake he drove on the right side of the road.

The drivers of these Conestoga wagons often smoked cigars made of homegrown tobacco, which became known as "stogies."

Goods from John Turner's farm and those surrounding it were loaded down at the Hazelwood docks or at the bottom of Brown's Hill. Items that could be dried or cured—like ham, dried pork or corn—were taken to Pittsburgh. There, the merchandise was loaded onto boats packed with other trade goods like whiskey, glass, pig iron and nails, and exported to the Caribbean after the boat hit New Orleans.

It's a safe bet that no one in Squirrel Hill would guess that the biggest change yet to come would occur because of something everyone took for granted—black rocks you could find everywhere.

Coal was so plentiful in the Ohio Valley that it could be mined just by chipping away at exposed layers in the hillsides. Because it was so easy to gather, people used it to heat their homes, and this lent a dense gloom to the morning air as a thousand houses sent coal smoke through their chimneys. The "Great Pittsburgh Coal Seam" averaged eight feet in width and covered 8.5 million acres, stretching to reach four states. The mountains that held this layer of bituminous, or soft, coal were also packed full of oil, natural gas, limestone, clay and iron ore—the building blocks of the Industrial Age. Some creeks were so full of these substances that if you stirred the water and lit a match, you could actually ignite a faint mist over the stream.

When Pittsburgh was officially declared a city, the easy availability of these natural resources began the city's transformation from a farming community to a place full of people who worked for other people. Boatbuilders, blacksmiths, wheelwrights and tanners hired apprentices and expanded their operations. Stores near the Point carried a plethora of locally made goods: watches, furniture, barrels, saddles, clothing. Sheet iron was manufactured in a rolling mill, the thunderous sound of the nail factory announcing the creation of a thousand nails a minute. Children often staffed Pittsburgh factories, and the new cotton mill had nine of them, ranging in age from seven to twelve years old, working full time.

East of the city, at the edge of a hundred-acre meadow, was Negley's flour mill, the first in the west to be run by steam. There was even a powder house—an ammunition factory—near the Turner farm.

Peter William Eichbaum was running Isaac Craig's and James O'Hara's glassworks on the South Side of the Monongahela River, and the factory was booming. Distillers demanded bottles to sell whiskey and beer, and wealthy homeowners wanted windowpanes. Other mills opened. Glass became an important line of goods. Jobs in the factories were physically demanding, but there were plenty of young boys to take on the grunt work, standing next to the furnaces to open and close the molds while the blowers made the bottles, or carrying trays of bottles back and forth through the hot mill.

My dad left school when he was real little. He used to have to blow glass in the mill. He was very, very young.

Though the Shadyside iron furnace failed within a year, new plants sprang up to take its place. Christopher Cowan ran a sheet-iron rolling mill, and Jeffrey Scaife opened a tin and sheet-iron mill at the corner of Fourth and Market near the Point. When the War of 1812 became imminent, iron surpassed boatbuilding to become the town's leading industry.

By all means make your first approach to Pittsburg in the night time. Around the city's edge and on the sides of the hills which encircle it like a gloomy amphitheatre, their outlines rising dark against the sky, through numberless apertures, fiery lights stream forth, looking angrily and fiercely up toward the heavens, while over all these settles a heavy pall of smoke. It is as though one had reached the outer edge of the infernal regions, and saw before him the great furnace of Pandemonium with all the lids lifted... In truth, Pittsburg is a smoky, dismal city, at her best. At her worst, nothing darker, dingier or more dispiriting can be imagined. The very sun looks coppery through the sooty haze.
— Willard Glazier, "The Great Furnace of America"

Smoke from Pittsburgh's coal-driven factories combined with smoke from household coal furnaces to create a deep, lingering smog. Since roads to and from Pittsburgh were improving, it was easier to commute, and there were now quite a few factory owners who could avail themselves the luxury of a country home. More and more wealthy families were leaving the city for rural areas like Shadyside, Squirrel Hill or Hazelwood where the smoke was less intrusive. Many a Squirrel Hill farmer's wife was feeding her cows within spitting distance of a stately mansion.

Negley's flour mill stood at the corner of Penn and Collins avenues in Point Breeze. Since Penn Avenue was then part of the Greensburg Turnpike, the mill was in a perfect location for Negley to transport his goods.

Oakland was named after Peter Eichbaum, whose last name means "oak tree" in German. He lived where Montefiore Hospital is now.

Settlers who relocated from the more sophisticated areas of New England and Virginia were appalled by the rough lifestyle led by most residents of the Ohio River territory. Back east, there were real houses, not rude log cabins. Most Pittsburghers didn't know a carpet from a bed, since a log cabin bed was likely a blanket on the floor. Their clothing was washed only occasionally, if at all. Men didn't cut their hair; they tied it in a rough ponytail that ran down their back. No one except the very rich seemed to know what a fork was. Despite Hugh Henry Brackenridge's tenacious campaign, when it came to lifestyle, it was still hard for someone from back east to tell a settler from an Indian.

In Scotland, even so-called common people were religious and educated. Pittsburgh's Scotch-Irish residents were determined to continue that tradition in America, leaving a trail of churches and schools behind them. Brackenridge had already helped found Pittsburgh Academy, a school for ten- to twelve-year-olds at the corner of Cherry Street and Third Avenue. The building itself was rustic—desks were hung on the log cabin walls so they could be lowered when the schoolmaster slept there at night. But it was a beginning.

The settlers on Squirrel Hill didn't worry about amenities. Life was hard, and they had no time for such nonsense. There were fields to plow, animals to tend, water to tote from the spring. They had to feed their children and take care of their sick. Any illness could be devastating. When a girl from Cincinnati came to Pittsburgh with a case of cholera, with no hospital or sanitation system to contain the disease, 44 people died in less than a year.

Susanna Turner showed her Scotch-Irish roots when she persuaded her husband John to donate land to the town again. This time they would build a school. Common schools, as the public schools were called, were looked down upon by the rich, who thought of them as a place for poor children. It was true—hard-working settlers who could read and write had neither the time nor the energy at the end of a long day's work to teach their children themselves, and they couldn't afford to pay a private school's tuition. Susanna's and John's gift provided an opportunity for education to the children of their growing town.

Pittsburgh Academy was later taught by four Presbyterian ministers and a Roman Catholic priest and called Western University of Pennsylvania. It eventually grew to become the University of Pittsburgh.

Meanwhile, down south, Robert Fulton, a civil engineer who had invented the submarine some years before, was now embarking on a new project. He had a revolutionary design for a boat, one that could run both upstream and downstream. His partner, Nicholas Roosevelt, traveled to Pittsburgh to oversee construction of this latest invention. The New Orleans, a 150-foot steamboat, was launched that spring and it was a great success. Steamboat production began in earnest. Benjamin Henry Latrobe arrived to supervise the work at various locations, including the Browns' shipyard in Hazelwood along the Monongahela River. Eleven locks and seven dams would be built during the next twenty years to stabilize the unpredictable Monongahela for the steamboats.

There was also another new, exciting way to travel—the Portage Railroad.

> **The boats were drawn by horses through a magnificent tunnel 900 feet long—being cut through solid rock nearly the whole distance—and passes through some of the wildest scenery in the state; the axe, the chisel and the spade having cut its way through forest, rock and mountain. The valley of the little Conemaugh River is passed on a viaduct of the most beautiful construction... When viewed from the bottom of the valley, it seems to span the heavens, and you might suppose a rainbow had been turned to stone.**
>
> *— Charles Dickens*

Until now, the U.S. Army had been easily thwarted, since British ships could move much faster than the Army could on land. The American military drew up plans for a system of canals along the eastern seaboard, and construction began on the Portage Railroad. When it was finished, tavern talk between canal boat drivers and stagecoach drivers was consumed with which was the best transportation from Philadelphia to Pittsburgh.

The Clark's Ferry Bridge is now a highway bridge connecting Harrisburg to points north.

A trip on the Portage Railroad was complicated. You boarded a canal boat in Philadelphia, then sat in a chair on the upper deck while horses pulled the vessel onto a rail car and down to the town of Columbia, Pennsylvania (between Lancaster and York). Mules towed you through a canal that ran parallel to the Susquehanna River to cross the Clark's Ferry Bridge, an aqueduct at the mouth of the Juniata River. There it went into another canal that ran parallel to that river. When you reached the Allegheny Mountains, you saw before you a series of inclines. Your boat, with you on it, was pulled out of the water and through the forest, climbing each incline in succession until it reached the summit. After a stop at the Lemon Tavern, a second series of inclines took your boat down the other side of the mountain to continue the journey on another series of canals— a good time to take a nap in one of the sleeping rooms below. Eventually you ended up at a canal that ran alongside the Allegheny River. You passed through Stringtown and Allegheny City, then your boat was dragged by horses over a bridge above the river and through a tunnel below Grant's Hill to—finally—the Monongahela River and Pittsburgh.

The road that cattle drivers used to bring their cows to Pittsburgh to market is now called Beechwood Boulevard.

John and Susanna Turner are buried in the cemetery next to the Mary S. Brown Church on Beechwood Boulevard. The two headstones are level with the ground, their lettering now smoothed away by wind and weather.

The land owned by the Irwin family included what is now the intersection of Forbes and Murray avenues.

The Flowers farm stretched from Flowers Avenue in Hazelwood to Emahlea Street on the border of Greenfield.

John and Susanna Turner's nephew, John McCaslin, was very close to his aunt and uncle. When he married, they gave him and his bride Priscilla their two-story home. The Turners moved into a smaller log house along the wider road through town, the road that cattle drivers used to bring their cows to market. Herds of cattle made their noisy way up Brown's Hill, past Killymoon's Inn, then down past the Turner cabin on their way to Salt Lick Road, Braddock's Field Road and to Pittsburgh.

A few years later, when Susanna passed away, John Turner buried his wife in the family graveyard where his mother was laid to rest. He made out a will, naming his neighbor, Thomas Sutch, as executor, and leaving the bulk of his estate—113 acres of land—to John and Priscilla McCaslin. John Turner passed away seven years after his wife and was laid to rest next to her in the cemetery he donated to the town.

The McCaslins remained on the farm John and Susanna left them. The Turners' niece, Susie Halstead, married David Irwin II, one of the Dusters. Their nephew Turner Blashford got his own farm nearby and, though he did well financially, he suffered severe bouts of depression. During a walk along the river at the mouth of Four Mile Run, he took his own life.

The mayor of Pittsburgh, William Barclay Foster, had more troubles than simply running a growing city. His teenage son, Stephen, was driving him crazy. The mayor was wealthy—he made his money in real estate—so he could afford to support his family in style. They moved from their home in Lawrenceville to upper-class Allegheny City. They had the best clothes, and their children went to the best boarding schools. But no matter what he did, Stephen spent his time lollygagging with the Negroes who worked for his father, playing guitar and swapping songs. When sent to stay with his cousins in Hazelwood, he spent his entire visit playing their piano and making up tunes. By the time he was 18, he started to get some of his songs published, which gave the mayor some hope that he wouldn't have to support his son for the rest of his life. Stephen Collins Foster even settled down enough to marry a Pittsburgh girl named Jane McDowell, and two years later his song "Oh! Susanna" became a big hit.

The Fosters weren't the only prominent family with a wayward child. The Croghan family had come a long way since George Croghan ran his little trading post, and they were now "society." William Croghan, seeing a need to cloister his boy-crazy 15-year-old daughter Mary Elizabeth, sent her to a boarding school on Staten Island run by a Mrs. McLeod, known for diligence in keeping her girls away from boys. However, Mrs. McLeod neglected to keep the girls away from her brother-in-law, an AWOL British soldier, and 43-year-old Edward Schenley won Mary Elizabeth's heart.

Captain Schenley eloped with the teenager, and she became his third wife.

Mr. Croghan literally had a stroke when he heard the news, but the attack was mild enough that he managed to call the U.S. Navy to ask them to intercept the ship his daughter and her new husband boarded, bound for England. The newlyweds eluded the Navy by changing ships in Bermuda and made their way to England undetected. When they arrived, Edward was sent back to his post in Dutch Guiana to help negotiate the end of the slave trade there, and he and his adolescent bride moved to South America.

Meanwhile, back in Pittsburgh, a fire broke out at half past noon one day at Second and Ferry streets along the river. It had been two weeks since it had rained, and the dry weather took its toll. By six o'clock 1,500 houses had burned to the ground. Bakewell and Pears' glassworks, one of the largest of the 40 glassworks in the city, was gone, and so was the Douglas iron works and the Globe cotton factory. Many of the smaller stores and homes were burned beyond repair, but most of the mills and even some of the smaller stores and the numerous saloons were left intact. Members of the Third Presbyterian Church climbed onto its roof and covered the eaves with wet rags, preventing the fire from spreading there. Miraculously, only one woman died in this horrific blaze, though there were many injuries, and one dedicated fireman was burned so badly that his face bled. When the fire was ended, the oldest part of the city had only three houses left, and the rest of the town's 6,000 inhabitants stood huddled among the cinders.

The need for a hospital was apparent, and the Catholic Sisters of Mercy started one within a year. Challenged with treating a smallpox epidemic and three cholera epidemics within a few years of their opening, the Sisters gained a reputation for selfless devotion. Giving up their own beds to smallpox patients when even maintenance men were afraid to enter the building, these brave women saved hundreds of lives.

Disease was not the only threat to bodily harm. Factory and mill work was hazardous, and labor strikes could be just as bad. Until now, strikes had been orderly and ordinary—shoemakers had gone on strike nearly 50 years before, and printers had organized the city's first official labor union. But eight cotton factory workers were arrested and sent to the penitentiary after a strike that ended in a riot. City firemen were replaced after they went on strike and let 35 buildings burn to the ground. So when the puddlers and boilers at the iron works went on strike to protest a pay cut, management was on the defensive and sent representatives to find outside workers to break the strike. Eventually the militia had to be called in, and the men were forced back to work at a lower wage.

As industrial as Pittsburgh now was, most of the land in the rest of the Ohio Valley was still forest. Even in the city, nearly all the businesses were bunched together at the Point. To "move to the country," you merely had to pass Grant's Hill.

John George Woods had left Tullymet, his country home in Hazelwood, and his brother Harry moved there with his wife, Rachel. Harry Woods was sheriff for a time and used his influence to have Braddock's Field Road paved with wooden planks, making Hazelwood much more accessible from the city. As soon as the road was done, he planted a huge peach orchard behind the house and took out an ad in the paper to sell the remaining "vineyards, gardens and country seat." Pittsburgh's elite now had the opportunity to consider building country homes on this vast farm overlooking the Monongahela River.

Benjamin F. Jones, a young man who worked on the canals, bought himself a little piece of land at the end of Saline Street near Scotch Bottom. Jones had a good head for business, and when he saw the popularity of railroads in Baltimore, he figured canal travel might be on its way out. He figured that, if railroads were the wave of the future, there was going to be a boom in the sale of iron rails.

B.F. Jones worked at an iron works for a year to learn the ropes, then got together with Bernard Lauth to create the Jones & Lauth Company. A year later, Lauth sold his partnership in the company to a Scotch-Irish Presbyterian from Belfast named James Laughlin. They built their Eliza Furnace, Pittsburgh's first successful blast furnace, along the Monongahela River between Four Mile Run and Pittsburgh, near the Soho Rolling Mill. The location placed them between the mines in Connellsville and the city of Pittsburgh, where they could sell their products.

B.F. Jones was right, and soon folks were traveling from Philadelphia to Pittsburgh by rail. The trip took only fifteen hours and was much more comfortable than any other mode of transportation over land. Tracks were soon laid all through Pittsburgh—in the city's downtown, they went right through the center of Liberty Avenue.

Pittsburgh was rapidly rebuilding. The structure that would house the city's first department store, Horne's, was going up along the Allegheny River. The first high school was built, bringing the total of public schools to twelve and providing work for a hundred teachers. Bakewell, Pears and Co. rebuilt their glassworks. Samuel Kier, B.F. Jones' old boss on the canals, built a petroleum refinery— the first in America—near the corner of Grant Street and Seventh Avenue. Gas lights illuminated the streets and hotels. City council passed an ordinance to create a police department to replace the night watch. Pittsburgh was truly becoming a city to be reckoned with.

The son of Pittsburgh's former mayor, however, was sadly proving to be the disappointment his family had feared. Everyone seemed to be singing Stephen Collins Foster's songs, but there were rumors that Foster himself was digging through his pockets in a New York rooming house, trying to find the money to spend another day drunk. His wife Jane had left him and taken their daughter. It was rumored that Jane was being courted by an ambitious young Scot, a railroad man. His name was Andrew Carnegie. ♦

7 | THE IRISH

My dad would light his pipe and say, "I smoke my dudeen and curse the Irish," and my mother would respond, "That's 'cause the Johnny Bull's already cursed." The Johnny Bull's the nickname for the British.

Until the 19th century, the Irish emigrants to America were those who could afford the passage, which meant they were mostly Protestants from Northern Ireland. Irish Catholics, who were considered to be of a different race and were referred to in Ireland as Native Irish or Celts, had just recently been freed from a century under Ireland's Penal Laws, and were collectively poor as church mice.

WHAT WERE IRELAND'S PENAL LAWS?

A decade-long insurrection in the 17th century led to the deaths of thousands of Protestants and was followed by a retaliation in which thousands of Catholics were massacred. This British victory led to the Penal Laws, which forbade Irish Catholics from:

- living in a town or a city
- voting
- practicing their religion
- teaching
- attending school
- sending their children away to be educated
- selling newspapers or books
- owning land
- renting any parcel of land for more than one generation
- renting land worth more than 30 shillings a year
- owning a horse worth more than 5 pounds
- practicing law
- owning a gun
- serving in the military

Does this sound reminiscent of the oppression of Blacks in America? Consider the fact that peasants were often whipped by their landlords, and peasant wives and daughters were summoned to warm their landlord's bed. American slaves, who lived under heinous conditions, ate better and lived in larger, better-ventilated huts than Ireland's Catholics. An Irish Catholic peasant living under the Penal Laws actually had a life expectancy lower than that of an American slave.

The Penal Laws were repealed in the mid-19th century, but hostile treatment of the Irish Catholics continued. A horrifying example of this is the British reaction to the potato famine. As much as one-fourth of Ireland's farmed land was used to grow potatoes, a staple in the Irish diet, so when a potato blight hit, it was devastating. The British response to this tragedy was to export what little food was left in Ireland to England. As a consequence, a million Irish starved to death. More than a million more—mostly peasants from the south and west who were able to raise enough money for the fare—left Ireland to look for a better life in America. It would be another decade before the poorer Irish could follow, clutching tickets sent by friends or family who had settled in America or by industrialists recruiting laborers to break strikes in their mills.

When immigrant families from other countries came to settle in America, the move was usually a process. The head of the family would move to the new country, decide whether it suited them, get established, and finally send for the rest of the family when jobs and housing were assured. Irish Catholic immigrants, however, were determined never again to return to British rule. Whole families left Ireland together, never looking back.

My mother was from Ireland, Donegal. She'd never cross the pond again. No, she'd never make that trip back to Ireland.

Travel conditions were so bad that 40,000 emigrants died on their way to America, either from diseases contracted on the voyage or because they were unlucky enough to have booked passage on one of the 40 passenger ships that sank in the Atlantic Ocean.

When the Irish Catholics moved to the United States, their economic station didn't change much. In Ireland, they were the poorest Irish; in America, they were the poorest Americans. Protestant Irish, who had already made a place for themselves in this country, began calling themselves Scotch-Irish to distinguish between themselves and the ragged Irish Catholics. Before long, the words "Irish" and "Irish Catholic" were synonymous.

When the Irish arrived on American shores, they had no money. Most were only trained to work as farmers, and farming was not a way of life they could easily pursue in the new world. In Ireland, small farms surrounded villages in a tight-knit community.

In America, farmers lived far apart from each other, which meant living away from a Catholic church.

My grandfather left Northern Ireland—there were Catholics in the north in County Tyrone—in his early 20s to go to England to work in the coal mines. A cholera epidemic had taken place in New Castle and they lost a lot of workers and peopled them with the Irish. He married a girl there, also Irish, and they came immediately to Johnstown. There were opportunities there in the steel mills.

In many cities, free Blacks had already moved up the economic ladder, and the Irish took their place in the jobs they left behind. House servants were typically Irish. So were miners and canal workers. Digging canals was an especially dangerous job because of the threat of disease. Malaria spread so rapidly among the workers that it was referred to as "canal fever." Railroad work was also dangerous, so much so that it spawned the frightening saying: "There's an Irishman buried under every railroad tie." And once the canal or railroad was built, a man was out of work again.

Irish Americans who lived together and worked together formed a tight-knit group. They had fought oppression before, and they knew how to organize to help each other. Organizations like the Ancient Order of Hibernians protected priests back in Ireland while they offered a clandestine Mass or administered sacraments to the sick and elderly. Secret societies had for years defended peasant rights in Ireland, and they weren't afraid of violence if it was deemed necessary. Here in America, unions like the Molly Maguires, an outgrowth of the Ancient Order of Hibernians, protected workers' rights, often with the same vigilante approach.

STEERAGE

Most new immigrants, not only from Ireland but from all over Europe, made their way to America in the cheapest way possible: traveling in the cargo hold of a ship.

These steerage passengers spent most of their two-week trip in the bowels of the vessel, seldom being permitted to walk on deck in the fresh sea air. Hundreds of men, women and children were crowded into a large room full of iron bunks—a straw-filled mattress, a blanket and a life preserver which doubled as a pillow— each berth separated from the next by an iron pipe.

Steerage passengers slept, ate and stored their luggage in their bunk. A fortunate traveler might have access to a washbasin filled with salt water, which would double as a bathing sink and a dishpan. Drinking water was often dirty, and few ships had a doctor on board. The primitive toilet facilities were usually not cleaned until the last day of the voyage, when they would be scrubbed in preparation for inspection when the ship reached port.

Like many other ethnic groups, the Irish paved their way to success by choosing a few occupations and concentrating their efforts in those areas where their strengths could shine. Due to their British enemies, the Irish had one advantage over other immigrants—they spoke English. Years of being forbidden literacy had an interesting effect upon these people—with no way to preserve their heritage with a written history, they had a strong heritage of storytelling, creating a culture in which charm and personality were cultivated and highly sought. This gave them an advantage in certain fields—entertainment, journalism, the labor movement—and one career that looked especially interesting: politics.

Because of the potato famine in Ireland and the unwillingness of the government there to help people when they were starving, when the Irish came here, they were determined that the government was gonna do everything, and gonna help people instead of let them starve. A lot of what the Democratic Party stands for today stems from that disaster in Ireland.

An Irish politician had the enviable ability to raise the status of his brethren. He could give government jobs to his fellow Irishmen and ensure preferential treatment by the police, tipping the scales back to counterbalance the discrimination the Irish experienced nearly everywhere they went. Having learned by hard experience to live outside the rules, their inherent distrust of government made them create a system within the system. Political "machines" grew up, where the law was "you scratch my back, and I'll scratch yours." Favors were granted because you were loyal to the politician and to the party. Former laborers became policemen and firemen. Businessmen who backed a candidate could rely on their bid being accepted the next time a road was paved or a bridge built. Everyone in the machine benefited.

Little Ireland was leveled by the railroad in the early 20th century.

The first Irish immigrants in Pittsburgh were a group from Mayo and Galway counties. They lived in a cramped settlement at the Point called Little Ireland which consisted of houses, a confectionery store, and a few hotels and taverns. Even with two or three families sharing a small house, or even a cellar or an attic, conditions were still a step up from life in a mud hut in Ireland.

Irish immigrants all over the Ohio Valley lived in quickly built housing under squalid conditions. A man who came home encased in coal dust after a long day of hard work had no running water with which to bathe. Many families, especially those headed by widows who lost their spouses in mill or mining accidents, filled their homes with boarders to help pay the bills.

Trash was made more quickly than it was disposed of, and piles of rotting refuse filled streets and alleys. Garbage breeds rats, and rats breed diseases. Cholera, smallpox and tuberculosis were regular visitors to any Irish ghetto, and the mortality rate was high. Survival was a fight, and medicines were usually unaffordable, which may have been a blessing since they often did more harm than good. Laudanum or Peruna, full of opium, were given for pain as mild as a headache, and cocaine wine was sold to soothe the nerves. Kopp's Baby Syrup did as it claimed—put your child to sleep easily— because it was loaded with morphine. And Bayer, the aspirin company, had recently developed a new medicine it advertised as "Heroin, The Sedative for Coughs."

Irish immigrants moved near Squirrel Hill Road to work in mills and mines. Though they were from various counties such as Donegal, Tyrone and Cork, their bond as fellow Irish Catholics helped them to fight their daily battles together.

Many of the new immigrants escaped their lot, at least for a few hours, in a bottle. For those who lived in the Ohio Valley, where liquor was cheaper than bread, whiskey often substituted for a miner's evening meal. Saloons thrived, as did an Irish pastime: fighting. Irish street gangs not only defended themselves but went out looking for fights. To an Irishman, a fight was just part of an evening out, as much for sport as to resolve conflict. In New York City during this era, nearly half the people arrested in a given year were Irish, most of them charged with drunk and disorderly conduct. Police vans became known as Paddy wagons because they were so often filled with Irishmen.

An Irish neighborhood was a tough neighborhood. With fathers working long hours and mothers busy with domestic work, children were free to congregate and cause trouble. Boys were encouraged to play outside from a young age, and taught to stick up for their rights. It was a mark of status for an Irish boy to be a good fighter, and even the girls knew who the best fighters were. And since they came from a country where a male child was considered a lad until he was 40, none of these boys were in any hurry to grow up and settle down.

By now the Scotch-Irish, having been in the United States for a few generations, had carved out niches for themselves as respectable citizens. The way of life of the new Irish immigrants seemed to verify their long-held belief that the Irish were a separate race, one that could not be assimilated into the American culture. The Irish seemed to confirm this themselves—though as a group they were strongly anti-slavery, they had problems getting along with nearly every other ethnic group. There was a reason for this, and it was a simple one: in the old country, if an Irishman met someone who was not Irish, that person was British, which meant they were a sworn enemy. Therefore, the Irish came to this country with generations of bitter distrust of anyone who was not Irish. Since they were quick to learn that, in America, the degree of whiteness of your skin could determine your place on the social scale, they used this information to their advantage and had the hardest time getting along with Blacks.

Ironically, the Irish culture and lifestyle was very similar to that of free Blacks. Both cultures admired storytelling and colorful language. Instead of working to pursue higher education, they gravitated to fields like entertainment and sports, especially boxing and, later, baseball. Both were working hard to pull themselves up by their bootstraps after a century or more of oppression to make a better life for themselves and their people. Other ethnic groups recognized the similarities, and their racial slurs reflected it. The Irish were called "niggers turned inside out" and Blacks were derogatively referred to as "smoked Irish." In most places outside his own ethnic group, an Irishman was no more welcome than a Black.

Though they fought long, hard struggles with poverty, even the poorest Irish family put money in the collection plate at Sunday Mass. Although only 17% of America's Catholic population was Irish, they made up 35% of the clergy. More than half of America's Catholic bishops were Irish. An Irish neighborhood was not just a neighborhood—it was a parish. ♦

A TRADITIONAL IRISH FAREWELL

May the road rise up to meet you,
may the wind be always at your back,
may the sun shine warm upon your face
and rains fall soft upon your fields,
and until we meet again,
may God hold you in the hollow of His hand.

8

MINES AND MILLS, FACTORIES AND FORTS

Andrew Carnegie's family moved north of Pittsburgh when he was 13. His dad had been a weaver, as were his father and grandfather before him, famous in their hometown of Dumfermline, Scotland for their skill with damask linen. But progress in the form of cotton gins and power looms had made their trade obsolete, and Andrew's father moved to Allegheny City to look for work.

The Carnegie family lived in an area called The Bottoms on the north shore of the Allegheny River. Andrew and his brother Thomas hung with the boys in a neighborhood street gang: Henry Phipps, Henry W. Oliver, Robert Pitcairn, David McCargo, Thomas N. Miller, Andrew and Anthony Kloman. They called themselves the Bottom Hoosiers.

Andrew's father contacted some local Scotsmen, and before long he had a job. He got Andrew hired in a factory job. Then a different factory job. Then another. Andrew was not happy working in a factory. The first time an office position opened up, he jumped at the chance and even went to night school to learn bookkeeping. If Andrew Carnegie had any say in it, it was office jobs for him from now on.

Before long, Andrew had another job, this time delivering telegrams. With regular deliveries to all the important firms in Pittsburgh, he got all the inside scoop on how business was run in the city. When he landed a job as personal telegrapher for the superintendent of the busiest division on the Pennsylvania Railroad, he put this information to good use. By the time he was 24, Carnegie had his boss's job.

More important than his new position at the railroad, however, was the money he was making on the side. Carnegie bought interests in companies, then hired the companies to work for the railroad. He and another Bottom Hoosier opened their own telegraph company, which, of course, soon had contracts with the railroad. Andrew, his brother Tom and some other Hoosiers invested in a few local iron companies, including the Iron City Forge that the Kloman brothers ran down in Girty's Run. After partnering with Carnegie, military contracts were pouring in and Iron City Forge soon had a larger mill in Lawrenceville. When their puddlers went on strike, instead of signing a new contract, management sent to Europe for replacement workers. This tactic dealt them a stroke of good fortune. One of their recruits, an immigrant named John Zimmer, knew the latest German techniques and worked closely with the Kloman brothers to update their mill. Before long, the Kloman/Carnegie mill was the leading iron mill in Western Pennsylvania.

The Irish families who had moved to Squirrel Hill and Scotch Bottom settled into the quickly built houses that had gone up at the edges of the farms and estates. Some of the men were hired on at Jones and Laughlin (J&L) or one of the other nearby mills. Others made their living in William H. Brown's coal mines.

A miner's work cannot be glamorized. Mining was hard labor, filthy and exhausting. A man might stand all day in cold water up to his knees in a dark and dirty tunnel while he swung his pick at the walls. On worse days, he might have to bend down for hours to cut his share of coal, or lie on his side in a tiny passageway chopping at the walls. A minor cave-in was considered all in a day's work, and a man caught in one was simply dug out of the mess. Since he was paid by how much coal he dug, he got up, brushed himself off and went back to work.

Miners' wives worked just as hard, if not harder. A woman was expected to tend the garden, take care of the children and make

Puddlers stirred the melted iron and removed the slag. This was a skilled job—they learned to judge by sight when the molten metal was ready.

One of the entrances to the coal mines, a bell-shaped building at the corner of Haldane and Connor streets, was converted to a home and is still standing. Another mine entrance was on Winterburn Street.

A cistern was a
family's water
tank. It was set up
next to the house
so rain that hit the
roof would collect
there. There was a
filter in the center
made of gravel and
broken bricks, and
the water would be
drawn from the
opposite side of
the filter.

clothing for the family. Lucky homemakers had a cistern. Those without one had to carry water from the nearest spring, and though spring water was good for drinking, if they wanted to clean with it, there was the added chore of softening the water with lye. When winter came, the home's primitive refrigerator was a hole dug in the garden, where the fall's harvest of parsnips, celery and cabbages was kept covered with straw to keep off the frost. Added to this, to make ends meet, many of these women also had jobs outside the home, cleaning and cooking at the nearby estates.

Poor children were expected to begin work at a young age.

My dad started in the mill when he was in third grade, can you believe it? Over at J&L.

Girls who had escaped from indentured servitude often hid out in nearby Pittsburgh, supporting themselves by working in the cotton mill or some other factory. Cigar shops, run from homes and small buildings, were staffed with children as young as six. The youngest would sit on the floor and strip the tobacco while the older children rolled it into cigars. They all worked long hours, and it was a familiar sight to spot an adolescent girl gently waking a little boy who had fallen asleep on the job, his little head cradled in a pile of tobacco leaves.

The boys in the cigar shops sampled tobacco in their off-hours, but rather than cigars, they preferred a new product—cigarettes—which offered trading cards with pictures of actresses in every package. The boys' fathers told them they looked like sissies with their newfangled cigarettes, and told them they ought to chew tobacco like a man.

Traffic to and from Pittsburgh was as busy as a modern freeway. Barges and tugboats trudged up and down the rivers, taking coal to the mills and finished products away to be sold. Little passenger steamboats dotted the waters. Four-mile-an-hour freight trains crossing busy Liberty Avenue caused horse-and-carriage traffic jams in the center of town. There was a regular stagecoach route traveling Braddock's Field Road by which you could ride from Squirrel Hill to Pittsburgh for ten cents. The same trip going ten miles an hour by boat was a lot less bumpy, but you had to pay for your comfort with a whopping 50 cents. Though the now-fabled Pony Express had come and gone, there was regular mail service between Pittsburgh and points east. Travel by steamer and buggy was so easy that, up the Monongahela River, the Kenny family opened their farm so folks could spend a day there having a picnic in the country.

Little towns were popping up, many of them named for the nearest industry. Pipetown grew along Braddock's Road, and farther down the Monongahela River toward Squirrel Hill was Frankstown, near the Frank Glass Factory. Railroads extended to meet these

TRAVELING BRADDOCK'S FIELD ROAD

Braddock's Field Road reached from downtown Pittsburgh to the site of Braddock's battlefield. The part of the road that went from Pittsburgh past Four Mile Run to Hazelwood is now called Second Avenue.

The route was sometimes called the State Road and it was a toll road, as were most of the main avenues leading to Pittsburgh. One tollgate was at the intersection with Brady Street. If you took the road as far as Six Mile Run and then wanted to cross the river, you had to pay another toll to ride the ferry. The Hays family ran this passage boat, which went back and forth from Six Mile Run to the upper part of Scotch Bottom, until the Glenwood Bridge was built in 1895.

Marion Coal Company was a quarter-mile from the railroad trestle at the corner of Second and Greenfield avenues.

Grove Station on the railroad was across Second Avenue from William Barker's mansion.

towns, and you could travel wherever the trains went at the unheard-of speed of 25 miles an hour. The Pittsburgh and Connellsville Railroad went right past Pipetown through to Glenwood. You could get on in Frankstown, at Marion Station by the Marion Coal Company, in Scotch Bottom, at Brown's Station, Laughlin's Station, Grove Station or Glenwood. In Hazelwood, the railroad tracks went through the center of town instead of their customary route along the river because the wealthy residents who lived along the water didn't want the trains to block their view.

When theater performances were interrupted one evening with the grave announcement that Fort Sumter had been attacked and the Civil War had begun, Squirrel Hill's Turner Rifles were ready and raring to go. Rather than serving together in a single regiment, they divided their forces among various military units. Pittsburgh residents were proud of their boys in uniform, but as soon as they left, panic followed. Folks were sure the city would be the target of a Rebel attack. Something needed to be done.

A meeting at City Hall determined that the threat to Pittsburgh was real, and the city should be ready to defend itself. Together with Secretary of War Edwin Stanton's newly created Department

MEMBERS OF MARY S. BROWN CHURCH
WHO FOUGHT IN THE CIVIL WAR

Charles & William Andre
John, Joseph & Walter Austin
D. Barclay
William Berry
Samuel Blair
Frank Bott
Samuel Brown
Joseph & Robert Cargo
James & John Clark
Jabez College
Harrison Craig
Jacob Delow
John Diller
Frederick Divner
Charles Ebdy
Louis Fleming
George Forward
George & Samuel Fowkes
George Goodworth
James Guthrie
James Hays
Adam Heckel

John Hepline
James Irwin
Donald Kennedy
Hugh, Lyle & William McCollister
O.S. McIlvain
Howard Morton
Alexander Murdoch
Jefferson & William Nelson
John Noble
Frank Ray
Adam Schaup
John Schmeltz
J.M. Schoonmaker
Robert Schull
Adam Shaw
Albert Smith
Charles Stewart
James Sutch, Jr.
A.B. Swain
Robert Ward
David Woods

of the Monongahela, a decision was made to build 27 forts in strategic locations throughout the area. Work began as soon as the ink on the governor's signature was dry.

Men were needed to build the forts, and the most eager young men had already gone off to war. A meeting was called of all industrialists in the area at which businessowners were asked to lend their workers to the war effort. They balked, and after some argument, a compromise was reached: if the Army would pay the workers, the businessowners would supply them. Nearly 5,000 men were so conscripted, and work began on the forts.

WHY WAS PITTSBURGH A THREAT TO THE SOUTH?

State-of-the-art iron-clad Navy warships, vastly superior to the Southerners' wooden ships, were built in Western Pennsylvania and powered with coal dug from the Great Pittsburgh Coal Seam. These vessels, armed with rifles and grenades, were responsible for the Northern victory over the Rebel Navy near Memphis.

The Union Army's munitions were made in Pittsburgh. Guns and ammunition were made in powderhouses scattered throughout the Ohio Valley, and nearby Lawrenceville was home to the Allegheny Arsenal, where cannons, shot and shells were manufactured. (This was exceedingly dangerous work: 70 women and girls who worked at the arsenal were killed in an explosion at the beginning of the war.)

They got some army people at downtown Pittsburgh, and if a healthy man was going down the street, they'd tap him on the shoulder and say, "You're in the army." And they gave him a pick and shovel and hauled him to a fort and put him to work. Just like that. That's how you got recruited into the army during the Civil War.

One logical location for a fort was along Squirrel Hill Road, overlooking the Monongahela River on a bluff called Mount Airy or Tunsel Hill. This fort was not to be a building but rather a breastworks, a breast-high trench from which fighting men could hide from bullets as they aimed their rifles over the rim.

Fort Black. It wasn't a fort as you think of a fort, maybe. It wasn't logs or anything, it was mounds of earth. And crevices and craters in there.

Nearly 50 men from Brown's coal mine were directed to dig the Squirrel Hill fort. They went at it with gusto. When they were finished, the miners needed help to climb out of their ditches, some of which were 15 feet deep. Of course, the trenches were completely

Murray Avenue was named after Magnus M. Murray, the fourth mayor of Pittsburgh.

Judge Walter Forward's house was near what is now the corner of Shady and Forward avenues.

unusable, and after an ear-beating from their supervisor, Mr. Chess, they had to dig two more small trenches shallow enough for a man to see over the top. Cannons were installed.

Old maps show the fort as Fort Squirrel Hill, but it was more popularly known as Fort Black, after a Colonel Sam Black who was killed in the Civil War. It was also referred to as Fort Lytle since it was on the Lytle farm, and Fort Chess after the man in charge of building it. Most fortunately, there was never a reason to fire the cannons.

All the factories and mills had made the city grimier and less pleasant to live in, so more and more wealthy folks were moving to homes outside the city boundaries. A trip down Braddock's Field Road during this era would take you past gatehouses poised at the entrances of long driveways that led to lavish estates. The country homes of the Squirrel Hill and Hazelwood elite were different, more wild than the manicured lawns and pristine mansions of Shadyside. Housing styles ranged from mansions to cabins, and nearly all were surrounded by untamed forests of oak, ash, wild cherry, spruce, chestnut and, of course, hazel trees.

Starting on the upper side of Braddock's Field Road traveling along the river toward Six Mile Run, the first country home was the stone house where the Woods family lived. Next was Hill Burgwin Sr.'s magnificent estate, followed by Captain James Nixon's place, the Hugert place, the Wiley farm with its log house and the Blair family mansion, which looked more like a castle. William Barker's mansion, The Grove, was also in this stretch. Where Chatsworth Avenue now stands were the homes of Henry W. Oliver, who was once a Bottom Hoosier, and George H. Anderson, secretary of the chamber of commerce. Down along the river was the beautiful brick house on the Scully estate, along with the Laughlin cottages, riverboat Captain William Robinson's house, the McCargo house— Mr. McCargo was president of the Allegheny Valley Railroad—and the Luckey mansion, home of the superintendent of city schools. The Scully estate reached from Braddock's Field Road to the river. Thomas Bedillion, the jeweler, also had a home in the area that he surrounded with a park complete with lakes, bridges, flowers and trees.

Wealthy people were also moving onto Turner's Federal Hill. Judge Walter Forward, secretary of the Treasury under President Tyler, built a country house not far from Saline Street, and John Covode, the Republican congressman who would later try to impeach President Andrew Johnson, lived near Murray Avenue.

Pittsburgh's borders already stretched to the edge of Schenley Farms, and the city began to incorporate all the small towns surrounding it in nearly every direction. Squirrel Hill was no exception, and the town was annexed and divided in two. The upper section, which was still mostly farmland, retained the rural name.

The more settled part of town now contained not only Turner's log cabins, the church and the school, but also mansions and farms and newly built little miners' cottages. To become a community of their own, they would need their own name. William Barker, Jr., a member of City Council who lived along a stream that emptied into Four Mile Run, was asked to christen the town. He called it Greenfield. ◆

9 | Machines

The city of Pittsburgh, meanwhile, busily gobbled up the towns surrounding it. Its borders now extended past Lawrenceville, Peebles, Collins, Oakland and Liberty, as well as encompassing twenty-seven square miles in Birmingham on the southern bank of the Monongahela River. Though the city was still predominantly Scotch-Irish, a full third of the population was new immigrants, mostly Irish and Germans who had been recruited by local industries.

The memory of the fire that nearly destroyed downtown was still fresh in people's minds, and local fire companies sprang up. Most of the firehouses weren't much more than a shed, but every company had its own colors and a mascot. There was a city ordinance requiring every home to have a leather fire bucket so every able-bodied man could assist if a fire broke out, but no one ever needed to enforce the law since the mere hint of fire would bring every man running from a mile around. The police had more work on their hands stopping street fights between the rival fire companies.

Downtown Pittsburgh was expanding, and cut after cut was made to flatten Grant's Hill. Even the skating pond at the base of the hill was filled in. Horne's Department Store was joined by Rosenbaum's and Boggs & Buhl, and Kaufmann's moved their store from Carson Street to downtown. To compete, Horne's hired a man to deliver packages for shoppers every afternoon from his wheelbarrow.

Of course, some might say it was hard to see all these improvements through the factory smoke, but your average working man didn't want clear skies. Smoke meant the mills and factories were running full tilt and, when Friday came, he would have a paycheck in his pocket.

The Peebles family had acquired quite a bit of land, including 75 acres of John Turner's Federal Hill property. Peebles Township included Squirrel Hill and Greenfield.

German immigrants were often referred to as Dutch. This comes from the fact that they referred to themselves by the German name for their people, Deutsch.

WHAT IS A BESSEMER CONVERTER?

A Bessemer converter purifies raw iron so it can be made into steel. The process is done in an enormous steel kettle, about 20 feet high, full of molten iron. Air blown into the bottom of the pot burns away the carbon and pulls out silicon and manganese to be removed as slag. This leaves the metal clean and ready to be formed. The converter was invented almost at the same time by two men, an American named William Kelly and an Englishman, Sir Henry Bessemer.

Jones & Laughlin now employed 2,500 men, and they were coming up against strong competition. Andrew Carnegie, who was just a boy when J&L was already a large company, was giving them a run for their money. Carnegie had a new mill along the river in nearby Braddock, named after a stockholder who was also, not coincidentally, president of the railroad. At this new plant, the Edgar Thompson Works, Carnegie took a gamble and installed a new invention he had seen, a Bessemer converter. It paid off. The switch was on from iron to steel.

While all this was going on, two Irishmen named Christopher Lyman Magee and William Flinn made their way sideways into Pittsburgh politics. Magee's uncle, Tommy Steel, was a little man with a hunchback, hardly your typical politician. But his sisters had married a couple of good-looking men—one a wagonmaker named Bigelow from Diamond Alley, the other a haberdasher named Magee with a shop on Wood Street. The Magees' son, Christopher, was a tall fellow with good looks and an easy demeanor.

When his father died, Chris Magee dropped out of college to help support the family. Uncle Tommy started Chris out working small jobs in the city and, by the time he was 23, Chris was elected city treasurer. Uncle and nephew worked together to create a "machine" to control city politics. Chris even went to New York City to study Boss Tweed's successes and failures there, and to Philadelphia to study the way their political machine worked.

The plan was simple. Chris, a likeable fellow, would get elected for a minor post—he chose fire commissioner—from which he would back men for City Council, men he could trust to do his bidding. It worked like a charm, and as soon as Chris Magee's men held a majority on the council, he began to control things from the outside.

It was at about this time that William Flinn came into the mix. Flinn was a successful contractor who had run for a city office and beat Chris Magee's brother Fred, whom Chris had backed for the post. When Magee found out that Flinn had won by getting his employees to vote for him, he decided Flinn would be an asset to the machine. Magee offered him a trade—city contracts in exchange for a guarantee of the Flinn employee vote. Everyone was happy, and the partnership began.

Magee and Flinn started a wild ride that would make them both very rich. They opened banks that loaned the city money at the highest possible interest rate, yet paid 0% interest on money the city deposited. Together with a couple of wealthy locals—Henry Clay Frick, whose family business was liquor, and A.W. Mellon, whose family owned a bank—they bought property on the main roads and then submitted improvement plans to their obedient city council. The contracting firm of Booth and Flinn had trouble keeping up with the demand for their work. City streets were paved in unprecedented numbers. Sewers were dug and tunnels were created to ease travel. Railroads, finding that bribes of money and rail passes would get them whatever street closings or other favors they needed, began to branch out all over the city.

Magee himself got into the transit business with Duquesne Traction, a streetcar line that went up so fast that Booth and Flinn had to drop their other work to complete it. When it was done, the

five-mile-an-hour mule-drawn trolley cars with their hay-filled floors were replaced with bright shiny new electric streetcars. With bridges and other work financed by the city, Magee was able to increase his initial investment of $1,500 to a whopping $30 million.

Vice, always lucrative in Pittsburgh partly due to the ever-increasing population of single immigrant men, was another profitable city endeavor. Instead of accepting bribes, the machine set up agencies. A house of prostitution or a gambling establishment could operate as long as it rented from an unofficial agent of the city. If they also bought their furniture from another agent, and their beer at twice the price from the machine's "official" beer distributor, the owner would never see the police at his door.

Despite these outrageous practices, Chris Magee was generally a well-liked man. His good looks and gracious personality worked well for him, and Pittsburghers were less concerned with how he did things and more concerned with what he did and how it affected them. Under the Magee-Flinn machine, dirt roads were being paved and a millworker could now take a trolley home after a hard day at work. There was talk about a city reservoir so residents could get water from a spout in their kitchen instead of walking to the spring or praying for rain to fill the cistern. And about using Flinn's company exclusively—why, if Chris Magee hired him, he must be the best contractor for the job! The one newspaper that dared to criticize Magee and Flinn, the Commercial Gazette, was convicted of libel with the added injunction that they were never again to mention either man's name.

This was not the only cover-up in the press. Local newspapers suppressed information about influenza and cholera epidemics, reporting instead of the healthful benefits of the smoke and soot that covered the city. Your eyes, they said, were more healthy because they had less strain since they were shielded from harsh sunlight. You had less chance to contract malaria since coal smoke would kill it before it could travel through the air. Mortality tables were published saying that Pittsburghers live longer than residents of other American cities.

> *My grandfather, he worked in the coal mines, and he died there 'cause he had black lung. He fell asleep in the mine and his lungs just stopped working.*

These arguments, however, were not convincing enough to keep the wealthy from moving to the country in their continuing search for clearer skies. Though many people still used their own horse and buggy for travel, railroads and trolleys made commuting from towns like Hazelwood easier than ever. Small businesses grew up near the factories and mills on the part of Braddock's Field Road that went through Hazelwood, lining the main thoroughfare with shops to serve the needs of the growing population. Henry Stahl had a grocery store, and there were blacksmiths and harness makers, pharmacies, a dairy store, a lumber yard, and even a theater, the Acropolis.

Contrary to what Pittsburgh newspapers reported, malaria does not travel through the air. It is contracted from a bite from an infected mosquito.

Shipping was big business in many towns along the Monongahela River, and Hazelwood was no exception. Captain Sam Brown and his brother Harry were the sons of William H. Brown, who, by the time he died, owned mines from Pittsburgh to Memphis to New Orleans. They lived near Nine Mile Run on a farm known as Brown's Hill and owned a shipyard in Hazelwood. Near the bottom of Hazelwood Avenue was another boatbuilding firm—Church, Keller and Swaine. Carpenters and river hands from the shipyards began to settle in Hazelwood and Greenfield alongside riverboat pilots like Captain Lytle and Captain Glasier. Hazelwood dockworkers were forever loading coal onto barges to fill factory and government contracts.

The Civil War was over now and the rich had gotten richer. Money plus leisure equals a good time, and where you found a good time,

you found Captain Sam Brown. He and some of the other men from the local estates started a private club that met at the Glen Hotel in Hazelwood. They ran horse races along Second Avenue starting at the hotel and ending all the way down at Three Mile Run. The racing parties, like the Turner Rifles' cork-and-gun club meetings over the hill, had the potential to get a little raucous. An example is the time Major John Williamson Butler, a retired military man from Greenfield, tarnished his reputation as a crack shot. He asked Joe Keating, the owner of the tavern across the street from the Glen Hotel, to toss his hat into the air so Butler could use it as a target. Butler promptly shot Keating in the cheek. Records do not show whether both were drunk at the time, but they do reflect the fact that the tavern owner wore that scar for the rest of his life.

When the smoke from the mills began to cover the skies over their country homes, wealthy Hazelwood and Greenfield residents moved to Allegheny City, across the Allegheny River from Pittsburgh. As they left for greener pastures, they subdivided the estates they had abandoned. Newly created streets were lined with hastily built homes rented to the flocks of immigrant millworkers recruited from Europe every time a strike was threatened. Some streets kept the names of their owners, others received Indian names: Susquehanna, Kennebec, Pocusset. One street was even named in honor of the Indian orator, Tecumseh.

The city's population had reached 85,000. There were now 32 schools in Pittsburgh, including a high school with 180 boys and girls enrolled. Settlers' children from farms in Greenfield and Squirrel Hill attended a school that looked a lot like a barn with shutters on its windows.

My grandfather built the house next door after the Civil War. He was an immigrant from Wales, and he spoke the language. His children were educated in the one-room school up here.

After school, the deep trenches of old Fort Black, now filled with water, made a terrific swimming hole—though a little bit scary because it was so deep. There was even a swing tied to a log set across the two head logs of the fort. In the winter, the man-made lake was a great skating rink.

Pittsburgh, like much of the country, was becoming more progressive. There were more than 300 telephones in the city. For the first time in over 40 years, Black men could vote. Wealthy Pittsburghers tried to set an example by becoming more "civilized." Their language became more delicate and reserved. Men wore mustaches or beards and carried a six-shooter instead of a rifle. They referred to a woman not as a woman but as a lady. Her legs and arms were not mentioned in polite company, and if they were, they were referred to as limbs. Topics for mixed company never included a woman's undergarments or even a man's shirt.

The working poor, however, had no time or patience for this folderol. Pittsburgh's population had nearly doubled in the last decade, and the new immigrants were busy working. There were more mills now, which meant more jobs to be filled. Along or near Braddock's Field Road—now the newly paved and renamed Second Avenue—was Jones & Laughlin's Eliza Furnace, Blair's mill, the Roller and Evenson mill, the Pittsburgh Bolt Company, the Frankstown glassworks and the Glenwood rolling mill. The old powder mill in Greenfield was still in operation, and National Tube had just moved their plant from East Boston to Western Pennsylvania.

Working men made an average of $1 or $2 a day, and their children made about $2.50 a week. The newest immigrants typically made less than those who came before them. Across the river, Slavic immigrants put in long hard days for ten cents an hour. Though some Pittsburgh industries were progressive—the workers in George Westinghouse's factory actually had Saturday afternoons off—at most of the mills, men worked twelve-hour shifts except on Saturdays, when the shift was shortened to nine. In desperation, nearly a dozen unions joined together to form the American Federation of Labor under the presidency of John Jarrett of the Amalgamated Iron and Steel Workers. Their hope was to better the dangerous working conditions and low wages of the working class. ◆

Squirrel Hill Elementary School was on Squirrel Hill Road at the corner of Tesla and Bigelow streets.

10 | A Neighborhood Begins

So here we are. Greenfield is now part of the city of Pittsburgh. How have things changed? Let's take a morning stroll down Squirrel Hill Road to find out.

We can start at the old Turner farm, up at the top of Brown's Hill. John and Priscilla McCaslin inherited this land from the Turners. They sold it to Joseph Bails, who sold it again, and now it belongs to Martin Beehner. Down the road a piece, if nobody's looking, we'll swipe a piece of fruit for breakfast from the Lannon's orchard. They won't miss it—they have row after row of trees full of apples, cherries, peaches, pears and quince, raspberry bushes and black currant bushes, reaching way down the hill below us.

After we're done eating our purloined fruit, we'll head toward Gardner's Spring for a cool drink of water. It seems odd to watch cows peacefully grazing in a meadow on one side of you, and find so much activity on the other. Across the way, women are hanging out their washing, row by row, in front of crowded clapboard houses. Their husbands stop to kiss them goodbye before they commence with their daily hike down the dirt road to the mill. Little children run past us, laughing, on their way to school.

Mule teams trudge by us, dragging wagons of coal from the mines to the mills, up the hill and down the hill and up again. All along the way, we say hello to miners. Coal mines line the road for nearly a mile, the long arms of the mine branching out toward the center of town.

Past Gardner's Spring is Edwin Collins' brickworks. A few years ago, the gas company was digging gas-line ditches on Collins' property when they realized the mounds of dirt piling up around them were actually thick, rich clay. The men put down their shovels and called their boss, who called his boss, who called some bricklayers. When Mr. Collins trudged up the hill after a long day's work at the Demmler Tin Mill, the bricklayers offered him a partnership.

Now, horse and wagon teams from the Squirrel Hill Brick Company deliver brick all over the city. Brick deliveries are slow, deliberate work. If there are a lot of hills on the way to the construction site, the wagon driver has

Lannon's orchard stretched from the fire house on Winterburn Avenue to Bigelow Street.

Gardner's Spring was at the corner of Bigelow and Bristol streets.

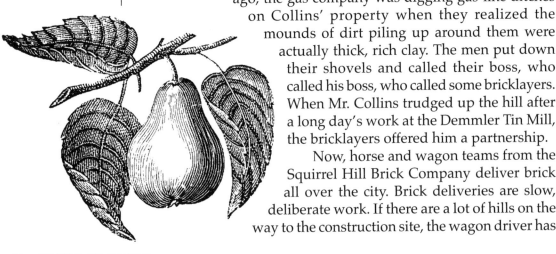

to bring an extra horse along to help. It can take all day to make a trip from Bristol Street through Schenley Park to an Oakland work site.

Collins, a tough Welshman who started out as a blacksmith down in Hazelwood, runs the brickyard. He named the streets that surround us in honor of his beloved Britain: Bristol Street, Gladstone Street, Chambers Way.

All over the city, steel is booming. Jones & Laughlin added 54 beehive ovens to their Second Avenue mill. Carnegie bought a mill in Homestead from Pittsburgh Bessemer Steel and installed a bunch more Bessemer converters and hired Henry Clay Frick to oversee the business. The glass-works are thriving, too—half of all the glass produced in America is made in Pittsburgh. New products are being invented all the time. Charles Martin Hall recently developed a new metal he calls aluminum, and the Pittsburgh Reduction Company is producing it. People think it looks promising.

Unfortunately, there is plenty of industrial progress but little being done to improve working conditions. They continue to be deplorable. Everyone in Greenfield is still terrified when the mill's whistle blows when it's not time for a shift change. Even little children know that's a signal to shut down operations because there's been an accident. If a man is maimed or killed, his wife and children get no compensation; most companies won't even pay hospital or funeral expenses. An accident is considered a hazard of the job, and you should know that when you sign on.

Every time the unions hold a strike to better the men's wages and working conditions, the company simply sends emissaries to Europe to hire more workers. When the mill owners caught on to the fact that the immigrants who replaced the union men were joining the union themselves, they started to recruit from different countries each time so it would be harder for the new immigrants to communicate with the men on strike. As soon as their Irish and German workers went on strike, management was on its way to Italy and central Europe to recruit.

Work in the glass factories isn't any better. Glass is now heated in a continuous tank instead of separate pots. "Continuous" means swing shifts for everyone, even the children. The glare in the factory is blinding, and most of the men have eye trouble. Conditions are so bad that some of the glassblowers are sending their sons to school instead of getting them jobs in the factory. More and more boys in the glass factories are orphans or sons of widows, children who are desperate for work.

Of course, there are a few extraordinary men like John Brashear over on the South Side, who works his 7-day-a-week, 12-hour-a-day shifts at the mill and then climbs the hill to his house to spend the rest of his waking hours building telescopes. Andrew Carnegie must think men like Brashear are the rule rather than the exception, since he built beautiful libraries near his mills and equipped each with a lavish music hall and luxuries like swimming pools and bowling alleys. Carnegie's upper management gets a lot of pleasure in these palaces, but the average working man who has slaved and sweated for the last 12 hours is only looking for a meal, a beer and a bed.

The saloon is often the only place these laborers spend their few precious social hours. Greenfield's beergardens, as well as all of the taverns surrounding the mills, are a welcoming place for a working man. He doesn't have to make himself presentable before he goes there, because the bar will be filled with dirt-covered men just like him. He doesn't have to worry about whether he stinks, because the smell of the bar will easily overpower any stench he carries.

Women don't enter these mill bars, and the men don't mind that they're filthy places. Some taverns even have a trough that stretches along underneath the bar so a man can relieve himself without stepping away from his beer. At these beergardens, a weary man can stop after work and have a drink to wash the dust from his throat, joke with his friends in his own language, and gather the strength to get up tomorrow to do it all over again.

Liquor is still a big business in Pittsburgh. There are more than 20 breweries around the city, and even priests and preachers have a drink or two—or three. Lately, the upper class is worrying about the lower classes' proclivity for drink. Local mill owners are more and more separate from the men they manage, and it's obvious they're afraid that one day the men they oversee will gather forces as a drunken mob, coming after their less-than-benevolent bosses. Wealthy industrialists sit in overstuffed leather chairs at their private clubs, sipping brandy from crystal snifters as they discuss ways to distract the working men and their families. They have already used their influence to get Pennsylvania to extend its "blue laws" to include saloons, so at least no drunken mobs will charge their Sunday soirees. But what about the rest of the week? Chris Magee's cousin, Edward Bigelow, just presented an idea that looks worthy of support.

Edward Bigelow was a city engineer before he was even out of college. When he became director of public works, he presented an ambitious strategy to City Council designed to keep the working poor in line. The plan was based on the theory that a beautiful city would bring out the best in people, that a poor man would choose a park over a bar any day of the week. Pittsburgh's elite were hopeful and gave the project their full backing.

Bigelow's first big coup was acquiring Schenley Farm, not far from Second Avenue's mills. The land had been in Mary Elizabeth Schenley's family since her ancestor George Croghan, the trader everyone called the White Mingo, received it as a grant from the government. The land had been passed down to William Croghan, Mary's father.

Though Croghan and his wayward daughter reconciled, his attempts to persuade her and Captain Schenley to move to Pittsburgh had failed. Croghan lived alone at Picnic House, his estate in Stanton Heights—occasionally amusing himself by throwing one of his famous stag parties—until he passed away, his butler Cox at his side.

Mary Schenley now owned the estate, and she was still living in England with no plans to return to Pittsburgh. Bigelow contacted her and was able to buy the farm for only $51,000 (though he appeared to have taken quite a commission—it showed up on the city books as $70,000). Mrs. Schenley also donated the land surrounding the old fort's blockhouse at the Point as well as a third parcel of land that would later become Riverview Park.

Bigelow put Greenfield's men to work building roads through Schenley Park. The Squirrel Hill Brickyard was temporarily closed, and they used the brickyard's horse teams and wagons. Energized by the sight of his dream becoming a reality, Bigelow began plans for another park further east and patched together Highland Park from more than 100 separately purchased parcels of land. When he went after local tycoons for further donations, Henry Phipps presented the city with a conservatory at the entrance of Schenley Park, and Andrew Carnegie established a museum and library there. Henry Frick donated a park to be named after him. Chris Magee and his buddies at Duquesne Traction gave the city a zoo.

But the "City Beautiful" movement did not play out as the industrialists had hoped, perhaps because of something they hadn't considered in their planning: the poor had no time to enjoy the parks because they spent all their time working. While wealthy families were picnicking on Schenley Park's Bowling Green, strikes at the mills got increasingly violent. When steelworkers at the Homestead Works struck near the turn of the century, Carnegie told Frick how to take care of things—lower the wage and break the union—and took off for Scotland. Frick had little sympathy for the striking workers. He had planned to do what he usually did when there was a strike—close the mill down for a few days and then open it

A statue of Edward Bigelow stands in the middle of the road across from Phipps Conservatory in Schenley Park. Bigelow Street and Bigelow Boulevard are named after him.

George Croghan's original land grant was more than 1,000 acres and stretched from Lawrenceville to Turtle Creek.

The origin of the term "private eye" came from the Pinkerton logo — a large eye with the motto "We never sleep."

The Casino was where the Frick Fine Arts Building now stands.

again with recruited strikebreakers. But discontent escalated to a fever pitch. It wasn't going to be so easy this time.

Frick built a tall wooden fence around the Homestead mill and cut holes in it, which the striking workers took to be gunwales. For a show of strength, he hired the Pinkerton Detective Agency, who sent some quickly recruited and poorly prepared mercenaries to stand up against the strikers. Subsequent riots around "Fort Frick" turned bloody, and the Homestead Strike became the Battle of Homestead. When it was over, though the strikers won the battle— they beat the tar out of the Pinkertons—they lost the war. The unions were debilitated, wages were cut and working conditions continued their downward plunge.

Well-to-do folks, meanwhile, immerse themselves in diversions from these unpleasant topics. Baseball, a sport created to boost morale after the Civil War, is becoming popular. Travel by steamship is popular, too, though steamships aren't the safest way to travel: they're navigated on a system of educated guesses about the depth and safety of the waters, and many of the captains—especially those on Sam Brown's boats—like to race, which adds the very real possibility that the boiler will explode. But steamships are beautiful and luxurious, bedecked from stem to stern with oriental carpets and oil paintings, illumined by crystal chandeliers and staffed with butlers and orchestras.

There is some affordable entertainment now near the museum and conservatory at the other end of Schenley Park. Andrew McSwigan, a former newspaperman, now works for Chris Magee, thinking up ways to promote his trolley lines. One is a chain of amusement parks that includes Luna Park at the edge of Oakland. The Casino, another attraction, burned down recently. It was a beautiful building made of wood and glass that even had an artificial ice machine. When it wasn't used for ice skating, it was home base for the Pittsburgh's hockey team, the Hornets. After the fire, McSwigan suggested Chris Magee make use of his old car barn on Craig Street. Magee built the Duquesne Gardens, named after his Duquesne Traction Company. The Gardens has an ice rink and an arena that seats 8,000 people. They host the Hornets' games now, as well as roller skating, boxing, operas, rodeos and nearly everything in between.

All the mill towns along the Monongahela are changing so quickly. One day, there is a farmhouse and stable surrounded by pristine forest; the next, there are rows and rows of cheaply made houses, their porches spilling over with millworkers, their families and their boarders. Stores are popping up everywhere to meet the needs of the growing population. The new J.M. Logan School on Lydia Street is teaching some of the children, which keeps Greenfield School's classrooms a manageable size. The Hays family no longer runs the Six Mile Ferry because the Second Avenue Traction Company built the new Glenwood Bridge so their trolleys could take workers over that route to the Homestead mill.

When Sam Brown's mother passed away, he contacted the Squirrel Hill Methodist Church and offered to build the congregation a brand new house of worship if they would name it after his mother. The church had blossomed since its humble beginnings in the log church the Turners founded, and they already had a large brick building. But they took him up on the offer and became the Mary S. Brown Methodist Episcopal Church. If you walk by, you'll notice that the sign reads "Methodist E."—legend has it that the stone-cutters weren't sure how to spell "Episcopal." Plenty of old local families besides Sam Brown's belong to the new church now, including the Sutches, Blashfords, Carrs, Castlemans, Davises, Craigs, Burchfields, McCaslins and Readings, and even two "colored" families, the Bronsons and the Clarks.

It seems like industries are changing daily, too. McKeesport's National Tube Works combined with 12 other companies, and it's now J.P. Morgan's National Tube Company. Carnegie Steel and a group of other companies including National Tube, American Tin Plate and Lake Superior Consolidated Iron Mines are now one entity—United States Steel, the world's largest steel corporation. Morgan bought U.S. Steel from Carnegie for $480 million. Carnegie, ever the philanthropist, gave away $325 million, keeping a mere $155 million for himself.

Squirrel Hill is still rural—only four people per acre—but everything else has changed. Scotch Bottom is gone. All that's left of Frankstown is a private social club that bears its name.

> Scotch Bottom was a wonderful little community between Hazelwood and Greenfield. It had churches, department stores, fine homes—it was a nice little village. Then Jones and Laughlin's come and built a steel mill. There was another town, Frankstown, the next town down the river toward Pittsburgh. A coke company come and took it, made a big mill. That ended Frankstown.

All that's left of Federal Hill, the farm John Turner got from his notorious brothers, is its name, assigned to a teeny tiny street that connects the old cow path that used to run by his house to old Salt Lick Road. The quiet forest land the Girty boys farmed is now a big city neighborhood. ♦

"Colored" was a term used at this time to refer to African-American people.

The Frankstown Club still exists today and meets in Greenfield.

11 | Religion and Hard Work

An Austrian, as listed on the U.S. Census in the early 20th century, could be one of any number of Slavic and Magyar peoples. The Austrian-Hungarian Empire in its heyday reached from Milan, Italy to Tarnopol in the Ukraine. Hungarians, Poles, Slovaks, Croatians, Lithuanians and others might call themselves Austrian.

Immigrants flooded through Ellis Island from impoverished countries around the globe, all with the same goal: to find work in the land of opportunity, the United States of America. For every four foreigners, three not only would work in the United States but stay and adopt it as their new home. Industrial cities all over the country were filling to the brim. Pittsburgh, with all its ready jobs, was a magnet for these newcomers. The city's population grew to nearly 350,000, with most of the new folk looking for homes near the mills and factories where they would work. Towns like Greenfield and Hazelwood chopped their rustic farms into streets and jam-packed them with quickly built houses. It seemed to the longtime residents that, almost overnight, a full half of Pittsburgh's population was from Italy, Russia and the Austrian-Hungarian Empire. Greenfield transformed from a Scotch-Irish town to a place where English was a second language.

Americans are often filled with fear and misunderstanding about their nation's latest influx of immigrants as they worry about how they themselves will be affected. Their worries are charged with emotion. Who are these new people living next door to me and my family? What are their morals? Do I want them to live in my neighborhood, to let their children play with my children? Are they willing to work for less money—will my employer hire them, could I end up without a job?

For fear to turn into prejudice, one important thing needs to happen: those who are feared cannot be seen as individuals but only as a group. Since America's new immigrants came from different nations and spoke different languages, to create a prejudice against them all, there had to be another unifying characteristic. One was found—the countries they came from were Catholic. The United States was swept with anti-Catholic propaganda, much of it originating from an organization called the American Protective Association. Though most of the APA's members were Republican, they had no qualms about attacking William McKinley as he ran for president on the Republican ticket when it was suggested that he might be a Roman Catholic. Their membership was so widespread that, by implying that McKinley was merely a frontman for the bishop, the APA nearly cost him the presidency.

There had never been any great love in Greenfield between Protestants and Catholics, though violence was usually confined to little boys throwing stones at each other.

Well, I can remember that Presbyterian family lived down the bottom of the street. Then I think the one married a Catholic and that's how they got into the Catholic section.

Protestant Irish lived up this way. Wouldn't you know they'd be up on top of the hill. Where the cannons could kill everybody.

Part of the problem, as is usually the case, was simply that they didn't get to know each other. People naturally tend to settle where they are most comfortable: near people from their native country, close to the church where they worship. Greenfield was full of little separate communities, each in its own pocket of the neighborhood.

Protestants who were descended from the town's first settlers lived on top of the hill along Bigelow Street, the old Squirrel Hill Road. The Welsh families attended Hazelwood Christian, the Baptist church over the hill. When there were enough of them—17 adults and 10 children—they formed a little congregation of their own, holding services at the homes of Robert James and Edwin Collins while they built a frame church on Bristol Street. When the congregation grew, the church was replaced with a new brick one at the corner of Gladstone Street and Squirrel Hill Road. It cost a whopping $10,000.

Irish Protestants who lived among the Welsh on top of the hill attended Hazelwood Presbyterian Church until they had enough members to start their own congregation, Greenfield Presbyterian Church. Their first building was at the corner of Coleman and Mary streets, but within five years, their congregation grew enough to require it to build their own large red brick church.

Slovak immigrants, both Roman Catholic and Greek Catholic, gathered where Four Mile Run met the Monongahela River, in what was left of Scotch Bottom.

The Run even had a little Protestant organization, the Hope Mission, that offered Sunday school and held picnics and other social activities for Protestant children in the Run who had been displaced from Scotch Bottom when the mill was built.

The town's Irish and Italian Catholics lived along Greenfield Avenue and worshipped at St. Rosalia Roman Catholic Church, which they built on the old Barker farm.

St. Rosalia Church was a little teeny building way back in the hillside. It wasn't on Greenfield Avenue, it was back out of sight.

Though named after the patron saint of Palermo, Sicily, St. Rosalia was run, like most churches in the city, by Irish priests. Father McEvoy and Father O'Flynn constructed a frame building at

William Barker Jr.'s mansion was on the land where St. Rosalia Church now sits.

The majority of Pittsburgh's Jews were Lithuanian, Rumanian, Polish, Latvian, Hungarian, Russian and German.

the bottom of Garrison Street where they lived on the third floor and opened the first two floors for a parish school. The local Catholic diocese sent Sister Madeline Dawson and her Sisters of Charity to teach the children, and the nuns made William Barker's old mansion into their convent.

Pittsburgh's wealthy were Presbyterians and, like many religious people, were convinced that their church was the only proper one—though they did make allowances for Episcopalians. Catholics and Jews, on the other hand, were at the very bottom of the social ladder. Neither expected to rise to a management job while working for a Presbyterian. It just was not done.

The Jews skirted this issue by running their own businesses, usually with family members as staff. Already, most of Pittsburgh's retail shops, groceries and delicatessens were run by Jewish families. Until recently, Pittsburgh's 40,000 Jews had lived almost exclusively in the Hill District, but now many were moving near Greenfield to its rural neighbor, Squirrel Hill. They founded a synagogue, Shaare Torah, while Murray Avenue was still a dirt road.

Americans—meaning the Scotch-Irish, Germans and others who had been here almost too long to remember where their grandparents were from—held the white-collar jobs. An immigrant from German-occupied Poland who spoke German had a chance, though slim, at a managerial job. But those who spoke Polish, Hungarian or any other language worked as laborers alongside the Blacks who moved north after the Civil War, and every other man who had been recruited to break a strike in a Pittsburgh mill or factory. They were Pittsburgh's working poor.

The men would gather around the gate to the mill at shift times, and straw bosses would choose their workers from the crowd. Immigrants would try to dress and look as American as possible so they would be picked to work that day. Some bosses came to prefer immigrants, since they were often willing to work for less money and would do anything they were told. The bosses knew immigrants were desperate for the money and would never, ever think of saying "That's not my job" the way an American might.

In the latest generation of Irish Catholics, there were plenty of young men who didn't want to work in the mills, and they didn't have to. An Irishman usually knew someone who knew someone who was a politician, and a lad could get put up for a city job like policeman or fireman or even a pencil pusher in city hall. Many of the young Irishmen who did work at the mill took the cleanest job they could find, even if it meant being paid less than the laborers. A youth who weighed metal or kept time got to wear a suit and went home earlier, and considered the trade-off well worth the difference in pay.

It became more and more uncommon to see a person born in America with an unskilled job in the mill. If a man was shoveling coke, it was likely he was an immigrant. With Blacks still so few in number, eastern Europeans or "Hunkies" were doing most of the grunt work in the mills. Laborers in the mills came to be known by a generic term: "millhunks."

They were Polish and Hungarian that worked in the mills, all that type of people. We used to call them millhunkies but you can't say that anymore.

The term "Hunky" refers not only to those of the Magyar (Hungarian) population but to anyone with eastern European ancestry.

A millhunk was a hardworking man. More than half the nation's structural steel was made in Pittsburgh and the little mill towns surrounding the city.

With no union, a millhunk shoveled coal 12 hours a day, 7 days a week.

All I did was go to work, worked fourteen hours a night. Sometimes on night turn we went out, I think it was five o'clock, then when the morning come, come home. Long hours.

Some of the mills had a policy of giving every other Sunday off, but a man paid for it later by working 24 hours straight on the alternate Sunday. Add to this a half-hour walk or streetcar ride to the mill—if the crowded trolley has room for you and you don't have to wait for the next one—and you've got yourself one long day.

No one could even attempt to deny that working in the mills, like shoveling coal in the mines, was extremely dangerous. In a single year, Carnegie Steel had 42 men die in accidents at work. Jones and Laughlin lost 28 men that same year, and National Tube 13. Payment from the company for funeral expenses ranged from the rare high of $100 down to the more common "not a cent." A man who was injured and had to miss work got no compensation at all; though 30 other states had workmen's compensation, Pennsylvania, the heart of industry, did not.

Once when they were changing stoppers, the crane dropped the old one just as it swung clear of the edge of the ladle. It fell on him, burning him and breaking his leg. At another time he failed to lower the stopper in time, and the stream of molten steel struck the edge of a mold as the train was shifted; it splashed onto the platform, burning his legs so severely that for six weeks afterwards he was unable to turn over in bed. It is a common thing for metal to fly... the sparks strike his face, they lodge in his nose or his ears, and once he nearly lost the sight of an eye. He refers to these things as trifles.
— *John A. Fitch, "The Steel Workers"*

Those who weren't injured walked away with chronic health problems. Most millhunks were partially deaf from the constant noise of the machines. Shoveling coal into a furnace 12 hours a day in a shirt drenched with sweat gave them colds in the winter and dehydrated them in the summer. And the mineral dust in the air filled a man's nose and throat, leading many to stop for a medicinal whiskey on their way home.

Now, for an American man who worked in the mill, things were a little better. Management and foremen had plenty of perks. You worked shorter hours. You weren't dirty when you came home. And there were other advantages that were less obvious but common just the same, like getting on your wife's good side by sneaking out a man from your crew to help her with the spring cleaning.

If an immigrant learned to speak English, he might get the opportunity to work his way up to a skilled position. Landing a job in the yard meant only working ten hours a day, or even less depending on the time of year. Working with the Bessemers was an eight-hour day, with a day off every single week. Machinists worked a shorter day, too—except when something broke down. If there was a problem, the machinists worked until it was repaired, no matter how long it took.

Some would argue, many rightly so, that a millhunk's wife worked harder than her husband. If his shift started at seven o'clock in the morning, she got up at five o'clock to have breakfast on the table at six so he could eat in time to catch the trolley or walk to work. She spent the rest of the long day caring for their many children—birth control was nonexistent then and, even if it were available, most of them were Catholic and wouldn't use it anyhow. She cooked and cleaned for the family and whatever boarders they may have. Scrubbing clothes and diapers on a washboard in a tin tub, she often took in more laundry to give the family a few extra cents for food and rent. At the end of the long day, she made sure her husband and children had the best dinner she could manage on whatever money they had, then went to bed exhausted as soon as the dishes were done—which was often after her husband had gone to bed. A lucky woman had daughters at home to help her, but more often the girls married young and started homes of their own or were out working themselves.

For the young people who were working, things were slowly improving. Pennsylvania finally passed a law for a minimum working age—a law New York had passed 30 years before. This new law stated that boys under 16 and girls under 18 could only work nine hours a day, though they were still allowed to work swing shifts. It wasn't much, but it was movement in the right direction. What it would mean in the long run was more important—nearly every child could go to school, at least for a few years. ♦

12 | The Italians

My dad's side of the family came to America in the late teens. They weren't real open about why they came. I guess it was the reason everybody came, for a better life.

Mezzogiorno literally means "middle of the day."

Until the middle of the 19th century, there were really no Italians in America, because there was no Italy. The country that is now Italy was a collection of smaller countries, each with its own dialect and customs. From north to south were Piedmont, Venetia, Lombardy, Emilia-Romagna, Tuscany, Marches, Latium, Abruzzi and Molise, Campania, Apulia, Basilicata, Calabria, Sicily, and to the west Corsica and Sardinia. From north to south was the way the economy went, too, with the northernmost countries being the richest and the southernmost the poorest. There was very little emigration—for a time, it was forbidden—and when people did leave the country, it was often simply to France or Germany to do seasonal work and then return. Those who crossed the ocean more commonly went to South America than to the United States.

When Italy unified in the mid-19th century, the northern Italian economy improved even more. Like in Ireland, Italians from the north sought to distinguish themselves from southern Italians, whom they considered to be members of an inferior race. This snowballed into a caste system in which inhabitants of each country thought they were better than people from any country south of their own.

Natives of Italy did not see themselves as Italians. They saw themselves first as a member of their family, then a member of their village, then a member of their province. The customs of each village and province were different from the next.

Southern Italians from the Mezzogiorno, the six provinces east and south of Rome, were *contadini*, peasant farmers who put food on their landlord's table as well as their own. The land they tilled was often in a malaria-infested valley, forcing workers to live on surrounding hillsides, which added the toil of walking to and from the fields each day.

Like farmers all over the world who depend on Mother Nature for their livelihood, Italians from the Mezzogiorno believed in luck and fate. Some villages didn't even use the future tense in their language. The Catholicism they practiced included ways to placate evil and to appeal to saints to intercede on their behalf.

As many as 70% of Italians were illiterate, not because they were not smart—they were—but because formal education was not respected in an Italian community. Education in proper behavior was an important aspect of family life, but schoolwork was considered an intrusion into the family, an attempt to make children think differently from their parents. Laws passed in Italy to demand that youngsters attend school met with resistance ranging from simply ignoring the law all the way to riots and arson.

The first group of Italians to settle in Allegheny County—600 of them—joined the Jewish immigrants in the Hill District. When southern Italians did emigrate to America, most left with the idea of earning money for a few years and then returning home, and more than half of them did just that. Those who stayed long enough to be eligible for citizenship did not always apply for it, and many did not even bother to learn English.

When I was younger, my great-grandmother lived with us and she didn't speak any English, just Italian.

Italians in America continued to have a disdain for formal schooling. In New York City, a comparison study was done of education levels among various immigrant groups. While 16% of Jews and 15% of Germans had graduated from high school, 1% of Irish had graduated, and no Italians at all. If a son was patient, cautious, and in control of himself, if he respected his elders, he was considered well educated. The Italians used to say, "Only a fool makes his children better than himself." A son who would rather go to school than work was ridiculed, and a daughter who would rather study than help her mother was a bad daughter.

Rispetto—hard work—was valued highly. Talent came from God, so a man could take no pride in it, but hard work was a thing of honor. Like other immigrant groups, Italians concentrated on occupations in which they excelled. Many of the southern Italians started small businesses in trades they had back home as *giardinieri* (gardeners) and *calzolai* (shoemakers). *Giornatieri* (laborers) helped to build highways and railroads. Some were successful at working their way up to foreman and, after a generation or two, started their own construction companies. Fruit and vegetable peddlers, after a generation or two, became grocery store owners. Waiters and chefs had sons who eventually owned restaurants.

My grandfather had a landscaping business when he was just starting out. He had a horse and buggy. Going up Forbes Avenue, everything to the left was just one or two houses and lots of land owned by rich people. He used to take care of the yards.

The perception of Americans, however, was that Italians were not willing to work hard. Early on, there may have been some truth to that. Southern Italians had been oppressed since they were taken as slaves by the ancient Roman Empire. Local nobility had crushed them as best they could, and for generations they learned that initiative was more likely to be punished than rewarded. Perhaps it took a while to see the opportunities in America. But real or imagined, the perception was there, and the Italians were paid accordingly. When they arrived in this country, the jobs they got paid less to an Italian than they did to an Irishman or a Black man. They were at the very bottom of the economic ladder.

Status for an Italian, however, was not determined by the type of job held by the head of the household, but rather by the well-being of his family. Fathers concentrated on earning the daily bread and making the family's decisions. Mothers managed the family finances and raised the children. Fathers disciplined the children at the request of their mother.

So the Italians, like the Irish, brought a distrust of strangers to the new country. To an Italian, the most important bond was loyalty to your family and to those with whom you were blood kin, especially on your mother's side. Second was to the godparents chosen by your family. Third was loyalty to those from your village. The strong loyalty Italians have to their village is described in their word *campanilismo*, which comes from the word *campanile*, which means steeple. In the center of each Italian town was a bell tower. It was said that nothing of interest happened outside the range of the bell's sound. Anyone too far away to hear the bell was a stranger, which meant they could not be trusted.

When Italians moved to Greenfield, unlike other Italian settlements in the city where most of the immigrants were from the same province, they came from various provinces, brought together in the neighborhood in search of work.

Though the Italians learned to get along with other ethnic groups, it was most difficult for them to get along with the Irish. Though they were both Catholic, there was a very strong difference in the way they worshipped. With the Roman Catholic Church in America dominated by Irish clergy, many Italians felt they had no freedom to worship in their own manner. In some towns, they were even expected to sit in the back of the church, or politely told that they should find another parish at which to attend Mass.

St. Rosalia was always Irish, we always had Irish priests there. The Italians moved into Greenfield and they became, uh, a little bit perturbed because all we celebrated were the Irish occasions and the Italians felt left out, you know.

Very few Italian men became priests. Though the Irish invariably sent their children to parochial school where they were taught by Irish priests and nuns, Italians were often more comfortable teaching religion in the home, where they could instill their own beliefs and values in their own way.

Many Italian customs differed from those of their new neighbors. Italians drew a very distinct line between the roles of males and females. Girls learned to keep house as soon as they were tall enough to wash dishes at the sink. Education was especially frowned upon for them; though they might have a job, most would not even think of having a career. That would mean betraying the family by spending too much time away from them.

Daughters were kept at home under the watchful eye of their father and brothers. Most were not even allowed to leave the house unless they were accompanied by a female relative. Even as children, boys and girls did not play together—girls played with girls and boys played with boys. Southern Italians especially put a high value on chastity. Their illegitimacy rate was extremely low, and Italian prostitution was almost unheard of.

To an Italian, the manliness of a son was shown not by bravado but by self-control. An Italian boy should seldom drink enough to be drunk. He should avoid fighting as much as possible, delivering instead a very polite but very firm warning to a potential opponent. Thus, when finally provoked to fight, he would take it very seriously and plan to win by any means necessary. An Italian man who carried a knife or a gun might use it. It was hard for these new immigrants to mix with Greenfield's Irish, for whom "let's fight and then have a beer" could be a typical Saturday night.

Italian social life centered around the family. When children married, they were expected to marry other Italians. They would typically live in the same neighborhood as the wife's parents, and were expected to show up each Sunday for dinner with the extended family. The absence of a family member at a holiday, religious celebration or anniversary was frowned upon. As with the Irish, divorce or even separation were extremely rare. Problems were taken care of within the family. An Italian would never seek aid from the police or a charitable institution—to do so would bring shame upon the family.

Italian immigrants at this time had lower crime rates than most other immigrant groups, and the crimes they were involved in were minor infractions such as gambling. Organized crime did exist in America, but it was run by Irish and Jewish immigrants. ◆

13 | The Slovaks and The Run

The story of the Slovaks begins long, long ago while Jesus Christ was teaching his apostles in the far-off part of the Roman Empire called Jerusalem. The place that Greenfield's Slovaks would one day call "the old country" was then a mountainous land coated with pristine forests filled with wild animals. Roaming tribes of Celts— the same tribes that would one day come to Greenfield and call themselves Irishmen—called this country home. Hundreds of years went by before the Celts were forced out by new tribes, Germanic tribes invading from the north. They in turn were conquered by the Huns as they swept across Europe. Three centuries after that, the first Slavic tribes arrived from the east, banded together to form the Empire of Samo and captured the region that would be called Slovakia.

Slovakia became part of the Great Moravian Empire, which also included Moravia, Bohemia, Silesia, and parts of Hungary and Austria. The country was changed forever when two Greek missionaries, St. Konstantine and St. Methodius, converted these Slavic tribes to Christianity. Slavic priests were ordained, and Slovak joined Greek, Latin and Hebrew as a liturgical language.

When the last king of the Moravian Empire passed away, Magyar tribes from Hungary invaded and took over Slovakia. Slovakia remained part of Hungary for a millenium, while castles and basilicas were built and fell, cities grew and universities were founded. The Magyars made Bratislava their capital throughout the religious wars that ensued when they were threatened from the south by Turks.

While Slovakia was occupied by Hungary, the Slovaks were no longer allowed to speak their own language. Fiercely proud of their heritage, they refused to comply with this edict and kept their language alive by secretly speaking it at home. Around the fire, late at night, grandparents passed on the stories they were told when they were children. These were exciting and lurid tales, guaranteed to bring squeals from the children and promise nightmares for all. They passed on legends of the old castles in the region and their rulers. They told of forest creatures who were human by day and wolves by night. They told of rulers like Csejte, who, in her pursuit of eternal youth, bathed in the fresh blood of young girls.

Like the Irish and Italians, Slovaks tended small farms or worked as artisans in villages. Each town had its own style of dress to distinguish it from its neighbor. The way a woman's *babushka*, or scarf, was tied or the colors threaded through the bright flowers embroidered on a man's shirt told a Slovak which village a person was from.

At the center of each village, literally and figuratively, was the Catholic Church. Children went to Mass before starting their school day. The village priest was a leader in the town, and the nuns wore the traditional black garments and lived in old-fashioned convents.

The 19th century was a time of change for Slovakia. Anton Bernolak and Ludovit Stur standardized the Slovak language, the way Noah Webster did for Americans at the same time across the Atlantic Ocean. Slovakia's first primary schools were created, and a Slovak underground strengthened as it plotted to claim the country again. These political struggles led to mass oppression of Slovaks in the Hungarian Empire.

English, Irish and German immigration rates fell in America; at the same time, the steel industry was exploding. It wasn't difficult for American coal and steel companies to convince men in Slovakia that life would be better in the United States than in their oppressed land. Thousands of Slovaks left the forests and mountains of their home for the forests and mountains of Pennsylvania—to work in Pittsburgh's mills.

> My grandfather and my dad and his family were all coal miners. They all ended up in the mill. The mills were building up in those days, so everyone wanted to go into the big city.

Allegheny County was the center of American Slovak life during the early 20th century. Slovak newspapers and books were published in and around Pittsburgh. When the Slovak underground was successful, and Slovak and Czech representatives got together to sign the documents that would officially pull them away from Hungary to create the sovereign nation of Czechoslovakia, the treaty was known simply as the Pittsburgh Agreement.

Most of the Slovaks who came to Pittsburgh had been farmers in the old country. They were untrained, spoke little if any English, and were hired for the hardest, dirtiest and lowest-paying jobs in the mines and mills. They worked alongside immigrants recruited from other countries in middle and southeastern Europe, spending their days underground in the coal mines or shoveling coke in the steel mills.

It was true that jobs were plentiful and it was easy for men from eastern Europe to find work. One advertisement in a Pittsburgh paper actually specified, "Syrians, Poles and Romanians preferred."

It was common practice for a conqueror to forbid the inhabitants of a vanquished country to speak their own language. Besides acting as a demonstration of power and domination, it had a practical purpose as well. If it were illegal for people to speak their own language, it would be more difficult for them to secretly organize a revolt.

Slovaks were known throughout Europe for their fine craftsmanship as tinsmiths.

Unfortunately, some were hired specifically because of their lack of language skills and understanding of American hiring practices. When there was a job opening, a new immigrant might be told that the custom in the United States was to sell jobs. When the price was paid, a cut went to the foreman, and the immigrant was hired. Some gullible eastern Europeans paid as much as $10 to $25 for a job that paid 15 cents an hour. U.S. Steel insisted that it was their practice to immediately fire any foreman who was caught perpetrating this scam. Nevertheless, it did go on.

Hazelwood was full of Hungarians, so to live near the mills without being next door to their recent enemies, many Slovak immigrants settled in Greenfield. The eastern part of Scotch Bottom where Four Mile Run emptied into the Monongahela became a Slovak community that was known simply as "The Run."

After a Slovak immigrant was settled in The Run and had made a little money, he or she would often "sponsor" family members to come to America. This meant they would pay for a relative's passage with the understanding that the person sponsored would work to repay the boat fare when they arrived in The Run.

> My parents came from Czechoslovakia, both of them, but they didn't meet until they were here. My mother's older sister sponsored her to come to this country, and my mother stayed with her. My father was a coal miner, and he was a boarder at their house. He was 20 years old and had already been here three years, so he had some money saved. He offered to pay my mother's transportation, which she owed my aunt, if they were married. My mother was only 17 at the time (laughs); she always said her sister sold her.

Like their Irish neighbors on the hill above, newly settled Slovaks also sent money back to family who stayed in the old country, their generous gifts often amounting to as much as half of their salary.

> Down The Run, they were all either Slovak Byzantine or they were the Slovak Roman. There were a few Italian families, just mixed right in there almost in the center, who used to climb the steps behind Greenfield School and go up to St. Rosalia's.

Roman Catholic immigrants from Slovakia who settled in The Run, as well as those in nearby Hazelwood and Oakland, could not join St. Rosalia Parish. Though it was a Roman Catholic church, its priests spoke only English, and many residents of The Run spoke only Slovak. This meant that, to make their confession, they had to travel each Sunday to attend Mass at St. Elizabeth's Church on Penn Avenue in Braddock, the only Roman Catholic church near Pittsburgh where Slovak was spoken. It is easy to understand that building a Slovak church in The Run became an early and important priority.

MEMBERS OF ST. JOACHIM'S FIRST CHURCH COMMITTEE

Frank Alexin	Andrew Marhefka
Frank Benkovsky	Michael Masley
John J. Bodnar	Andrew Onda
Joseph Bohachek	Imrich Rozboril
Frank Bohunicky	George Sikora
Albert Drgon	Andrew Soltis
Clement Kovalosky	John Somsky

The domes of St. John's can be seen from the Parkway East today, just beyond Oakland on your right as you travel from downtown Pittsburgh.

Slovak immigrants petitioned the Diocese of Pittsburgh, and after a few years, Bishop Canevin sent Father Joseph Vrhunec to establish a Slovak parish to be named in honor of the grandfather of Jesus. The first Mass of the new St. Joachim Parish was celebrated at Marquette Hall on the corner of Second Avenue and Rutherglen Street. By the following autumn, the parish had built its own church on the corner of Boundary Street and Four Mile Run Road. The parish grew quickly, and in just a few years, the parishoners built an addition to house the growing congregation.

Father Vrhunec began a Sunday school program taught on both Saturday and Sunday, the only formal Slovak schooling offered in The Run. After nearly a decade of hard work and planning, a Slovak parochial school was added to the community.

Slovaks who practiced the Byzantine rite, known as Greek Catholics, attended St. John Chrystostom Church on Saline Street. Like St. Joachim's, St. John's quickly outgrew their little church. Men from the parish took the old church off its foundation and carried it three blocks away to the other side of the rectory. They built a beautiful new church, topped with domes and golden crosses, in the same spot where the old church had been.

Forbidden to speak their own language in their native country, the Slovaks in The Run were determined that their language would live on with their children. St. John's used the relocated old church building for after-school classes to teach parish children to read and write Slovak.

St. John's used the old building as a schoolroom. After school, we used to go there to learn how to write Slovak. I still have a beginner's book that taught how to write the letters. It's almost like Russian but their accent is different and some of their spelling is different. And the same with Polish, they have more accent and more c's and z's, but if they speak slowly, I get it.

As its Slovak population grew, The Run began to look less rural and more like a village from the old country, with churches and its own main street, Saline Street, running through the center. There was just one farm in the valley now, the rest of The Run filling rapidly with housing for the new immigrants.

There was a valley where the Parkway is now, and that's where Leech's Farm was. When we were six or seven years old, we used to go there to look at the cows.

Stores on Saline Street were busy, especially on Saturday when the iceman delivered ice for the iceboxes and folks went out to get their groceries for the weekend. Customers came to the counter at the Eagle with grocery lists in hand, chatting with their neighbors while the clerk gathered their groceries from the shelves, set them on the counter and added their total in pencil on a paper bag.

Everybody went to the Eagle store, you should have seen that place on a Saturday night. The line at the counter was three to four people deep.

Like their Irish neighbors, the Slovaks had an appreciation for alcohol, and taverns were sprinkled among The Run's stores and shops. Slovak men could be found at one of these beergardens at the end of a hard day's work, clinking their glasses together and shouting "na zdravie!" as they belted down a drink.

Children stopped after school for penny candy at the great big triangle-shaped building in the center of town. One by one along Saline Street came a drug store, a bakery and butcher shops. The Run's business district spilled out onto lower Greenfield Avenue. Frank Civitate set up a shoe repair shop. The Cipa family opened a grocery, and so did the Pisanos, and Josephine and Sam Funaras. The Kanai family opened a funeral home in the Lipchiks' old house. The Butchcos opened a shop across from St. John's Church.

Despite this progress, The Run never turned into a big bustling town. It didn't want to. It was a village… and it was home. ♦

DOBRU CHUT: FAVORITE SLOVAK MEALS

MAIN COURSE

Halusky (noodles and cabbage)
Kielbasa (sausage, usually served with sauerkraut)
Halupki Kapusta (cabbage filled with ground beef or lamb and rice)
Pierogies (potato- or sauerkraut-filled dumplings)

ACCOMPANIMENTS

Bread spread with bacon grease or butter
Potatoes fried with grease and onions
Alcohol—wine or Becherovka, an aromatic liqueur

And please remember: if a Slovak neighbor, especially an older person, should come to visit you, they will at first refuse your kind offer of something to eat or drink. Be sure to ask again. The polite way to accept something in Slovakia is to first refuse it twice.

School Days

14

"Hold out your hands," Sister said, "you lied to me." She hit them till they bled, with a flagstick. I was in first grade.

Pittsburgh's Catholic immigrants had very strong opinions about their children's schooling. If the American government insisted that their children go to school, they wouldn't send them to just any school. Their children would be educated by their church, in classes where teachers ruled with an iron fist and taught them the same values they were taught at home. Parochial schools proliferated in and around Pittsburgh, and nearly 25% of the city's children went to Catholic school. Most of these schools were run by Irish nuns, with German nuns running a close second.

I was always a good speller. We had a line form along the side of the room, and if you stayed at the head of the line for a week you got a rosary. I had about six rosary beads, I used to win all the contests.

St. Rosalia's old school building was falling apart and the parish built its students a big red brick building that fronted on Greenfield Avenue. The modern structure had 12 large classrooms and even an office for the principal. The pastor, Father John Faughnan, recruited Immaculate Heart of Mary nuns to teach at the new school and bought a building across the street for their Mother Superior, Sister Loyola, to convert into a convent.

We had one nun in sixth grade, she must have been 75 years old—at least she seemed very old to us, but of course we were only twelve. This boy, he was a little wee kid, he used to get her so mad that Sister would chase him around the room. He'd get up on top of the desk and he'd hop from desk to desk and she'd run up the aisle with her rosary beads flying; they'd catch on the back of the seat, and she'd have to stop and unhook them before she broke them, all the time shouting, "I'll get you yet!"

There were 371 students in St. Rosalia School during its first year. St. Joachim Church built its own school at the corner of Saline and Boundary in The Run. Its students were taught by Vincentian Sisters of Charity, who made themselves a home above the school while the parish built a convent to house them.

The old convent for St. Rosalia School's Sisters of the Immaculate Heart of Mary is now the GO Center.

The convent for the Vincentian Sisters of Charity who taught at St. Joachim School was at 28 Alexis Street.

When Christopher Lyman Magee passed away, a reformer took control, but the Magee-Flinn ring was back in high gear when Chris' nephew Billy was elected. Mayor William Magee lived right on Greenfield Avenue. Any mayor hopes to make improvements in his own hometown, and Billy Magee was no exception.

It didn't seem fair that Hazelwood already had two trolleys—the #56 McKeesport and #57 Glenwood—each with its regular route down Second Avenue. So despite the fact that deer and pheasants were still running through its streets and backyards, Greenfield got its very own trolley, #58. Owned and operated by the Greenfield Avenue Railway Company—one of the plethora of trolley companies in Pittsburgh, nearly 200 all told—#58 traveled from downtown Pittsburgh, out Second Avenue, past The Run and up the hill along the avenue, taking shoppers and workers past the church and the stores and the mayor's house, then on to the top of the hill past the Beehner farm. In the summer, the streetcars—picnic cars, they were called—were open on the sides and never had to turn around. The operator would just move from the back to the front and start all over again.

The honeydippers who came around at night to clean the outhouses were looking for a new line of work. Hygiene, which had just become popular since the discovery of germs, was coming to Greenfield. Billy Magee had the city install water lines. The piped-in water was filtered, and thankfully, because of it, disease dropped radically. Residents started to install indoor toilets, often putting them in the basement in case they backed up—nobody really trusted the newfangled sewage lines. Some houses also added a shower in the basement. This was a real boon for the lady of the house, because now her husband and sons could enter through the cellar door after work to wash off the grime of the mills instead of tracking up her nice clean floors.

Flinn and his men had been busy with city contracts, and Pittsburgh's main thoroughfares were nearly all paved.

When I was small, there were very few paved streets, very few. Streets were just muddy roads. On a rainy day, you couldn't even walk through them. Just what they called main streets were paved, and they were all cobblestone.

The newest streets were covered in asphalt rather than the more common brick and cobblestone, because bicycles now shared the streets with horses. These cyclists—who of course were also voters—had been clamoring for a smoother surface. A gentleman named Arthur Banker had recently imported Pittsburgh's first automobile, a De Dion from France, so these asphalt streets would come in handy if the automobiles caught on. And catch on they did. Before long, the Gulf Oil Corporation was printing its first road map, charting Allegheny County. Pittsburgh began to cater to automobile travelers and even got rid of the tollgates on its bridges.

Greenfield's streets, like most of the streets in Pittsburgh's little mill towns, had grown quickly and haphazardly. Many of the roads were on hills and ravines that desperately needed grading. The old creekbed that ran down Haldane Street had houses on one side of the street with steps going up to their front door, and houses on the other side of the street with steps going down. The stretch of Bigelow Street on the side along the fort was a vast hillside of mud surrounded by mines. Winders Street was muddy, too, but at least it had a boardwalk over it. Parade Street was just more mud.

At least Greenfield's main roads were paved. Most of Squirrel Hill's main thoroughfares were still dirt roads. Even so, Squirrel Hill got its own trolley, the tracks laid through the mud on wooden ties. The Squirrel Hill streetcar traveled up Forbes Avenue and then down through Greenfield to Brown's Hill, where it crossed Brown's Bridge to Homestead to what seemed to be the destination of nearly every trolley in Pittsburgh: the mills.

The city of Pittsburgh was victor in a couple of political battles. The U.S. Board of Geographic Names was given the task of making sure that city names across the country conformed with one another. They had taken away the "h" from the end of Pittsburgh, having no idea of the clamor it would cause in the town. Now, after 20 years of fighting, Pittsburgh won its "h" back. The second fight was won against Allegheny City, which agreed to merge with Pittsburgh to become its North Side. The merger brought Pittsburgh's population to half a million people.

Downtown Pittsburgh had to be enlarged for its growing population, and William Flinn's men leveled Grant's Hill a third time, taking it down more than 30 feet from its original height. Though in the long run it was a good idea, it did cause problems for the buildings that were already there. The county courthouse had to add a staircase to its lobby so people could get inside, and the Frick Building now had two lobbies, their old one and a new one they had to build in what used to be their basement. Flinn's men carted the dirt from Grant's Hill up to Oakland and used it to fill in St. Pierre's Ravine alongside the Carnegie Museum.

When school was over, Greenfield's children, like children all over the city, prowled the streets looking for something to do before they had to go home for dinner, homework and chores.

De Dion automobiles were built by the firm of Count De Dion under engineer Georges Bouton. The car had a single-cylinder engine and looked very much like a horse carriage without the horse.

The current parking lot between the Carnegie Library and the University of Pittsburgh's Hillman Library is made of earth from Grant's Hill.

Mr. Clydesdale's paper store was on Greenfield Avenue where the Parkvale Bank is now.

My cousins lived on Connor Street, and we used to walk up Lydia Street from St. Rosalia's and play at Logan School before we started home for Hazelwood Avenue. It was a long trip.

There were no playgrounds in Greenfield. We congregated in the streets. What did we used to do for fun? Fight, fight. We used to rap on doors, knock on doors and run. What do they call that? Tic tac?

Boys, especially Irish and Italian boys, hung around in street gangs, congregating on Greenfield Avenue or in front of stores in their "territory." A few industrious youngsters delivered The Pittsburgh Sun and the Chronicle-Telegraph for Mr. Clydesdale.

Children seldom had their freedom long, since few went to school past the eighth grade. Everyone knew that if a boy's dad worked on the railroad, the boy would work on the railroad. If his dad worked in the mill, a boy would work in the mill. He would start out as a door opener or messenger and hope to get moved to a skilled job in a few years. There was no reason for a boy to continue his education, since everything he would need to know he would learn at the mill. Girls would marry young or be kept busy helping their mother at home with the cooking, the laundry and the boarders.

I went to the last grade, I think, eighth. I didn't finish half of it. I started to work when I was 14. I was an errand boy for a tailor, delivering high-priced suits. He was in the First National Bank Building downtown. I took the streetcar down to work.

It was not surprising that more than half the children in the two new public high schools, Schenley and South Hills, were born in the United States, and almost none were immigrants from the Austrian-Hungarian Empire. The president of the school board created a curriculum that encouraged trades to be taught to boys, while girls would be instructed in the ladylike arts of cooking, baking and sewing. Some of Greenfield's youngsters began to attend Schenley High School, walking the two-and-a-half-mile stretch through the park and then climbing the hill each morning to the enormous new school on Bigelow Boulevard and Center Avenue in Oakland.

Seeing the reluctance of some of his parishioners to send their children, especially unchaperoned girls, to a public high school, St. Rosalia's Father Faughnan optimistically added a parochial high school. He was able to recruit 26 boys and girls for the first freshman class. True to expectation, Sister Loyola's nuns were strict and especially kept a hawk's eye over their young ladies.

We were going to the prom and one of the girls had a low-cut dress. Sister took her handkerchief and pinned it on both sides and tucked it in the bodice. When we got outside, we all teased her and said, "Oh, you look so nice with your bib on!" She grabbed that handkerchief and tore it off and said, "You think I'm going to the dance like that?"

The first day of May was celebrated at both the parochial and public schools. At Logan School, children grasped ribbons hanging from the top of the flagpole, wrapping the pole as they danced around, and competing for lollipops or other sweet prizes. St. Rosalia's May celebration was a more solemn, though joyous, occasion—the crowning of the statue of the Blessed Virgin. The May Queen, a high school girl judged by the Sisters to be worthy of the honor, entered the church as part of a long procession. Wearing a white wedding dress, she would walk to the front of the church and adorn the Blessed Mother's statue with a crown of fresh roses as the choir and the children sang "Ave Maria."

The old Greenfield School, bursting at the seams, became an apartment house, and public school students from Logan, Greenfield, and Forward Avenue schools joined Greenfield School in a magnificent structure large enough for them all.

Wheatland Avenue is now part of McCaslin Street. The Wheatland Avenue Bridge went above Magee Field, connecting the steps going down to the playground to the steps across from it.

I remember kindergarten in old Greenfield School, way down on Greenfield Avenue, while they were building the new school. By the end of September, we all marched, two by two, up the steps and into the new building. We were amazed at the space in the new school, and the swimming pool, which was something we never had. There was a big auditorium with a big curtain across that we loved to watch open and close.

Older students planted trees on the steep hillside along the massive stairway that led to the new building. The impressive structure had 28 classrooms and was presided over by Principal Adda Mann, who made sure her girls wore skirts and dresses, and her boys were clean and combed their hair. Greenfield's population continued to grow, and Roosevelt School was built at the corner of Murray Avenue and Loretta Street for students from that end of the neighborhood.

When Wheatland Bridge was so old and rickety it was about ready to fall apart, Billy Magee had his men tear it down and level the ravine below it to make a ballfield. City workers planted shade trees along the town's sidewalks, another brainchild of Edward Bigelow. But any child would tell you that the best thing Billy Magee brought to town—better than Magee Field, better even than the beautiful new bridge to Schenley Park—was the merry-go-round. ♦

15 | Barnstormers and Prizefighters

It was as big as the merry-go-round in Kennywood, and it was free. They had all the painted horses and the ones that went up and down, and you got to ride and ride and ride. You never wanted to get off a horse, because you move your feet and you lose your seat.

The Schenley Park carousel was on the flat area near the intersection of Greenfield Road and Overlook and Panther Hollow drives, where the traffic light is now.

Mayor Billy Magee hired the Philadelphia Toboggan Company to build three carousels for Pittsburgh. Of course, one went to Schenley Park, just a short walk from the mayor's house. The brand-new merry-go-round was an incredible menagerie of 46 horses, deer, goats, giraffes, ostriches, kangaroos, lions and tigers flanked by four hand-carved chariots upholstered in leather. The animals paraded around the huge organ in the center of a 50-foot platform. This lavish carousel stood inside a structure nearly twice its size that held a lunch counter, picnic tables, and even men's and women's toilet rooms. Each and every painted scene and mirror on the carousel had its own hand-carved frame, gilded in silver. The three city merry-go-rounds—in Grandview, Riverview and Schenley parks—had over 200,000 riders that first year, opening on July Fourth and running clear through Halloween. They ran at 14 miles per hour that first year but afterward were slowed to a less dangerous eight.

Any summer night, you might find 200 people crowded around Schenley Park's merry-go-round. Folks from "down The Run" would walk up Saline Street to stroll across the beautiful new bridge. Giggling girls would congregate after school waiting for the boys to finish caddying their last round at the park's golf course. A caddy with tips in his pocket could score a few points by treating the girls to penny candy or soda pop from the stands surrounding the carousel.

Schenley Park became a center of social life for the community. Family picnics and Sunday school picnics were held there during the summer.

My mother and dad used to take us, and the next-door neighbor would take their three girls, and we'd walk over and have a picnic lunch and ride the merry-go-round all day. That was what you did on a Sunday. Then when it got dark, we'd all walk home again.

Kids walked to the large meadow at Schenley Oval on windy spring mornings to fly a kite or peek into the stables to see the horses. Families met to catch a harness race, quietly warning their little girls to stay away from the "bad men" around the racetrack.

The Oval, that used to be a racetrack. They used to have sulky races up there on Wednesdays. That was big entertainment. Didn't cost anything to see them run.

Weekend strollers bought a little something to eat at the large grandstand in the Oval or walked down to Panther Hollow. Boys fished in the lake while making faces at the sweethearts in their rented canoes. On special occasions, automobile races ran through the park, the rumble of the engines sputtering through the trees. It was an amazing thing—the most rustic and the most modern entertainments were together, in one place, and at everyone's disposal.

When motorized aircraft came on the scene, Schenley Park's Oval became Pittsburgh's first airport.

The first airplane I ever saw landed in Schenley Park Oval. The airport there was only half a mile long. The planes were very small.

Barnstormers, daring pilots who made their living as entertainers, lit at the Oval to perform in their "flying circuses." The gathering crowd, many of whom had never seen an airplane before, gasped at the plane's loop-the-loops through the sky. Adventurous spectators could pay a few dollars for their own trip to heaven, climbing in behind a pilot in his two-seater flying machine for a bird's-eye view of the park.

An afternoon walk, or a streetcar ride if a young man was flush or wanted to impress a girl, would take him beyond the Oval to Oakland. There, he could get a ticket to Forbes Field to watch the Flying Dutchman, Honus Wagner, circle the bases in his crazy bowlegged way. Or if he walked a little farther to Craig Street, there might be something going on at the Duquesne Gardens. A very lucky young man might be able to get a ticket to one of the Gardens' boxing matches where he could root for Pittsburgh's bad boy, Harry Greb, to win yet another bout.

Greenfield's men had never lost the rough-and-ready reputation they earned years before when John Turner had his cork-and-gun club. Already proud of their notoriety, their chests swelled with pride at the mention of their hero, Harry Greb.

Ever since he won his first professional fight by a knockout, every man and boy in Greenfield followed Greb's career. Harry Greb was the son of an Irish mom and a German dad. His dad had been trying to train him to follow in his footsteps as a tinner. He didn't

Harry Greb lived in the Morrowfield Apartments. The telephone book listed him as "Harry Greb, pugilist."

want his son to fight, but there was no stopping Harry. He was born to fight, and that's all there was to it. Why, Harry didn't even train—before a fight, he would spend the night in a bordello after his favorite dinner of hot dogs washed down with root beer. The guy just fought so much he was always in shape.

Harry Greb held the World Middleweight Championship title three years running. He won most of his 400 fights despite nearly every opponent outweighing him by 15 to 30 pounds. Harry was fast—newspaper reporters called him The Human Windmill—and he fought dirty. At a time when fighting dirty was a recognized part of the sport, Greb was thrown out of a spar with Jack Dempsey for being too rough. But Harry didn't need to break the rules to win. When he fought light-heavyweight champ Gene Tunney in Madison Square Garden, his first punch broke Tunney's nose in two places. Tunney, who was five inches taller than Greb and outweighed him by 12 pounds, spent a week in the hospital. Years later, Tunney compared boxing Harry Greb to sharing the ring with a wounded tiger.

Greb lost the sight in his right eye during a fight, but he memorized the doctor's eye charts so nobody would know and he could keep on boxing. He was tough and he was wild, and it seemed like every boy in Greenfield wanted to be just like him.

Yes, there were more genteel Greenfielders, and the Gardens had amusements for them, too. One night, they could hear the famous recording star Enrico Caruso sing his beautiful rendition of "Vesti la giubba" from the opera "I Pagliacci." Another night, the March King, John Philip Sousa, had his band belt out their latest rousing hit, "Stars and Stripes Forever."

A short streetcar ride downtown opened up another world of entertainment. The very first theater in the world to show only motion pictures, the Nickelodeon, sat right across from Kaufmann's on Smithfield Street.

My girlfriend talked me into playing hookey, and we went downtown to see Frankenstein *the day it opened. "Oooh," you should have heard them. "Oooh, oooh," you could hear folks out loud, they didn't want to see a monster. Oh, were we scared!*

Bustling department stores like Frank & Seder and Gimbel's had vaudeville theaters scattered in their midst.

On a special occasion, if a family could afford the time and streetcar fare, they could travel past the Homestead mill to the trolley park on the old Kenny farm. Kennywood had been transformed by

HOW DID A VAUDEVILLE ENTERTAINER FROM NEW ZEALAND COME TO BE BURIED IN CALVARY CEMETERY?

Eighteen-year-old Rose Stewart was a contortionist, an acrobat with the ability to twist her body into all kinds of unusual shapes. She took the stage name of Aguinaldo and traveled the world, playing in packed theaters and vaudeville houses.

Rose had toured Australia and the Orient by the time she came to the United States, where she headlined at Pittsburgh's Grand Opera House. Her popular show went without a hitch on Monday and Tuesday, but before the Wednesday performance, she came down with a fever. It turned out to be spinal meningitis. By Thursday morning, the young girl was dead—halfway across the world from her home, with no family or friends at hand to mourn her.

Performers from the Ringling Circus, passing through Pittsburgh, heard the sad story. Before they left town, they passed a hat and collected enough money to pay for her funeral. The inscription on her tombstone honors Rose from these kindly "brother and sister artists."

the Pittsburgh Railway Company. Andrew McSwigan left the Duquesne Gardens to manage the park, and it now boasted tennis courts, a bowling alley, croquet courts, a rifle range and—most exciting of all—a new amusement ride to accompany the Dips: a rollercoaster thrillingly called The Racer.

There was always something going on "down The Avenue" on cobblestoned Greenfield Avenue and its surrounding streets. Men traveled to and from work. Horse-and-wagon teams from local businesses made their rounds, occasionally pulling aside to let the streetcars go by. In the early morning while the lamplighter was putting out the street lamps, Mr. Kearns would be there with his horse and buggy, stopping at each house on his route and pouring fresh milk from large jugs into the housewives' milk pitchers. As the day went on, the iceman and the bread man made their rounds. The scissors man walked up and down the side streets with his grinder on a little cart, ringing his bell so everyone knew he was waiting to sharpen their scissors and knives or fix their umbrellas. Hucksters like Mr. Miller clip-clopped by with their horses and buggies, shouting, "Apples, fresh apples, bluuuuuueberries" or "Tomatoes, getcher tomatoooooooes!" The ladies of the house headed outside at the sound, chatting with each other as they pulled nickels and dimes from their apron pockets to buy fixings for the evening's dinner.

Mr. Miller came from the Hill District. He had a horse and wagon and he came to our house all the time. He came to my mother's house when she was a baby. "You was a little brat," he used to tell her.

Summertime was glorious. As St. Rosalia's church bells rang to announce the morning, children eagerly dressed to be the first in line for the pool at Greenfield School, a real treat during the hot, muggy days of summer. Though swimming didn't begin until a less ungodly hour, the line began soon after six o'clock outside the door behind the school.

We children collected all our pennies and nickels and dimes to get chimes built on top of the school. They rang once at the half hour, and on the hour they played a tune. We were so proud because we had helped get them.

Girls and boys swam separately on alternating days. Each morning, children shuffled excitedly as they counted their place in line to see if they were in the first group of 30 to get in. Once inside, they changed into the bathing suits the school provided and waved good morning to the school's coach, tall handsome Mr. McKee, who acted as lifeguard. All the while, the second group of 30 kids anxiously waited out back for their turn to swim.

Kids congregated at Fort Black, digging around for leftover parts of rifles and handguns or playing in the coal mines. When a 12-year-old boy from Graphic Street was killed in an accident at the fort, parents began to warn their children away. But kids are kids, so of course they still played there, often staying all day except to chase the iceman to swipe ice chips off the back of his truck.

All that upper part along Bigelow Street, there were no houses then, it was all Fort Black, and coal mines underneath. When we were at my cousin's house on Connor Street we used to play in the mine. We didn't go in very far because Mother and Dad said not to. We would play house at the entrance, set the table and talk with our baby dolls.

When we'd leave the fort, we'd have to climb up this hillside. You know how on the upper side of Connor Street, there's a lot of houses with steps going up to them? Well, that's the way that hill was, it was pretty steep. We used to climb up over that hill and then walk across the gunwales.

Dinnertime depended on which shift a child's father was working. If Dad was working night turn, the family would eat at three o'clock so he would have time to catch the streetcar to the mill. If Dad was on day turn, Mom would have dinner ready when the streetcar brought him back from work. After dinner, when chores were done, the children ran outside again to play.

Now that so many immigrant families had settled in Greenfield, nearly every street was full of children playing. Sons and daughters of the folks who lived in the mansions or on the few farms left in town played ball or jumped rope with the millworkers' kids.

The neighbor girls had a real nice dollhouse. It had a door and everything. Their mother had a great big kitchen and she had napkin holders. Her napkins were rolled up in them and she kept them in the middle of her table. I liked that.

We played street hockey but we used a beat-up tin can and a stick to hit it. If somebody got a ball, usually a tennis ball, we played baseball. Nobody had a bat, we just used a branch of a tree.

Every street had a hopscotch game scratched on the sidewalk with a "chalk-rock," usually a hardened bit of clay found in someone's front yard. Men coming home from the mill had to walk around little girls playing jacks on the sidewalk or little boys playing marbles.

We used to play hopscotch. We played jacks in the summer. Anybody who had a ball and jacks was really popular.

Boys would turn the rope while the girls did salt and pepper. The girls would say "salt and pepper" so you'd spin it real fast.

When evening came, kids congregated in the street or in a meadow to play It Tag or Run Sheep Run.

Oh, I can remember playing Run Sheep Run. We would meet over at Denmarsh, start over at the corner of Winterburn and run up and through the alley and down the street. Oh, we had fun.

If it was raining, whole families played checkers or Monopoly, keeping the screen door wide open, or playing on the front porch so they could converse with the neighbors next door.

I remember when Monopoly first came out. People went crazy over it. On Sunday they would start right after church. They had dinner and then they started a game. Eight or nine in the evening they're still in the same game. That's the way they played.

Carnivals were popular all summer long—a Pittsburgh man named Hugh Ward had invented a game he called Bingo that everyone was crazy about—but school picnics were the event of the season.

Our school picnic was always some time in June towards the end of the schoolyear, it was always on a Tuesday. My mother used to pack a great big basket and you had to get up real early. We met in school and went down the Greenfield School steps and crossed the street to the streetcar to Kennywood. Wild, crazy, oh, it was a beautiful day.

Each school had its own picnic. Mom—and Dad if he wasn't at work—would put a big lunch in a basket, dress the little ones and cart the whole family to the trolley stop. Girls fidgeted with their

Jacks was a children's game that came with a small ball and ten jacks, little six-pronged metal trinkets about the size of a marble. Players sat on the sidewalk and bounced the ball, picking up jacks with each bounce, first one jack, then two, then three, etc.

dresses and stockings while the boys tried their best to contain their excitement under their parents' watchful eye. The summer streetcar would arrive, the picnic car with benches straight across and no aisle in the center. Children and their parents would climb aboard, and the cacaphony of their voices rose to a crescendo as they rounded the bottom of Whitaker Hill and the first child caught a glimpse of the Speed-O-Plane in the distance. The grownups took their picnic basket to a pavilion where they could play cards and gossip while they charged the older children to "watch your younger brother," and the kids ran off to buy their tickets and stand in line for the first ride of the day.

The Fourth of July was the only day the mills were closed. In Greenfield, there was a huge celebration. The Stars and Stripes flew proudly off the wooden porches of the new immigrants. There were picnics and parties, and whole families walked "down The Run" to see the parade that went out Second Avenue. Dads bought sparklers for their children, and some even made a trip downtown to Chinatown to get big fireworks to set off in their yards after dark.

On the Fourth of July they always had a parade along Irvine Street, all the way from Greenfield Avenue to the Glenwood Bridge. It was usually politicians, of course, and there was always a band, then any soldiers from the First World War. There was always a big to-do on the Fourth of July, that was a great big holiday for us.

When autumn came and school began, there were other types of amusement. Mr. Carr took young Protestant men and women on outings called Christian Endeavors. Packing a bunch of young people into his rented truck, he would haul them out to South Park where they could meet young folks from other Protestant churches. A 25-cent entry fee bought an evening of dancing to records.

We loved to meet at my friend's house where she would play records on an old thing we called a Victrola, a phonograph. That's the only way we got music, there was no such thing as a radio then. Anyone who had a Victrola was well off. The records cost 25 cents each and, if you weren't careful, they broke; it was almost like handling glass.

Meanwhile, overenthusiastic Catholic boys caught fighting while loafing on The Avenue were collared by priests from St. Rosalia and dragged to the lyceum, a frame building behind the church, to box out their battles instead.

Some boys spent rainy days at Dad's workbench in the cellar attempting to build a radio with galena crystals, a condenser and a thin metal wire called a "cat's whisker." If they were successful, they could listen to Frank Conrad, a man who lived on Penn Avenue and broadcasted phonograph records from his garage, catch a blow-by-blow account of a prize fight from Motor Square Garden on

KDKA, or even take the radio upstairs to Grandma's room so she could hear the church services broadcast from Calvary Episcopal on Sunday morning.

When the first snow covered the streets, boys and girls were up long before their parents awoke, grabbing the first warm clothes they saw and running outside to play. Every family couldn't afford luxuries like gloves and boots, but that didn't stop their children from spending hours in the wet snow building forts and flying down the streets on makeshift sleds.

In the winter, one of our neighbors always made a bobsled—a sled in the back, a sled in the front, and a board connecting them. Eight or ten of us sat on that. We would take turns standing down at the bottom on Saline Street to see if a car was coming. Then we'd start at the top of Alexis Street and ride all the way down to the railroad.

We always wore dresses, we didn't have pants or slacks, and we had long underwear on underneath and woolen socks and rubber galoshes with buckles on the sides that pulled up over our shoes. You'd pull your stockings up over your long underwear, and they'd have all these lumps because your underwear got folded over.

Older youngsters walked arm in arm to Schenley Park and ice skated on Panther Hollow Lake. Stopping to get warm near one of the fireplaces in the boathouse, they'd take a breather on a wooden bench while they dug through their pockets to see if they had enough money to buy something warm to drink from the man at the counter. If not, they could still snack on the potato they brought from home and threw into the fire earlier.

If the family was short of cash one week, the evening often found a boy squatting at the entrance of one of the mines, filling his trusty bucket with enough coal to last until morning.

Streetlamps were on a pole, and they had a white wick with a shade over it. A lamplighter would come in the evening and light them, and in the morning he'd come and turn them off.

After dinner, while the same boy's family gathered in the front room and his sister sat at the foot of Mom's rocking chair getting her hair curled in rag strips, he could watch the lamplighter come by and light the streetlamps, then go to sleep watching the sky, pink from the mills, through the coal dust on his bedroom window. ♦

16 | Prohibition and the KKK

When my grandma was a girl during Prohibition, her family made wine in the basement. Grandma used to cover it up and take it in a wheelbarrow to people's houses and distribute it.

There was a guy had a speakeasy down The Run, back of the old Greenfield School. You went to his house, you got a drink in his kitchen.

SPEAKEASIES AND PROHIBITION?

Prohibition was instituted by an amendment to the U.S. Constitution that made it illegal to manufacture, sell or transport liquor. A **speakeasy** was a "secret" place to buy alcoholic beverages during Prohibition. They weren't really secret. In most towns, everyone knew where they were, including the police who did little to enforce the law and who might stop by for a few drinks themselves.

Many taverns converted into speakeasies during Prohibition and kept a thriving business. Regulars drank bootleg liquor or bathtub gin at the bar from coffee cups. Because serving alcohol was against the law, some taverns became private clubs where you had to know someone to get in, using a password or a secret knock.

Nightclubs became speakeasies, too, offering entertainment and dancing. They served coffee that could be spiked with bootleg liquor or bathtub gin if you requested it in a whisper (spoke easy) from the waiter.

The Prohibition Amendment was a miserable failure and was repealed after only 13 years.

Bathtub gin was an illegal drink consisting of either homemade moonshine or grain alcohol (which was available "for industrial use only") flavored with oil of juniper. Bootleg whiskey was made in a similar fashion and colored with sugar heated in a saucepan on the stove until it turned brown.

Even if they had wanted to, it would have been difficult to enforce the prohibition law in Greenfield. There was liquor any which way you turned. And if an occasional law-abiding citizen took it upon himself to call the police, there would be plenty of time to clear out before an officer arrived, since he would have to take a streetcar from the No. 4 station in Oakland.

Not everybody complained about the Prohibition law, because bootlegging was a lucrative endeavor. Greenfield Jimmy Smith, a pro ballplayer with a .219 lifetime batting average, was smuggling liquor for his team when he realized that bootlegging was his true profession. He moved back to Greenfield and got to work.

Edwin Collins' Squirrel Hill Brick Company, meanwhile, had become a big business. Nearly everywhere you turned, you could see buildings constructed with his brick: the new Greenfield School, Hazelwood's Gladstone School, St. Rosalia Church, even majestic Soldiers and Sailors Memorial Hall in Oakland. The brickyard now had nine horses in its barn, and Collins had a second brickyard in Somerset. Collins and his family still lived on Bigelow Street, but they now wore fine clothes and drove motorcars.

These motorcars were becoming popular among the elite, so the city responded with government contracts to improve the ease of travel with the new machines. William Flinn and his men built the grand Boulevard of the Allies where Water Street used to be, and the Liberty Tubes to connect Pittsburgh with the South Hills. They did a great job with the technical end of this tunnel, drilling their way in from either side of Mount Washington and meeting in the middle less than half an inch off center. But the work, like most labor jobs in Pittsburgh, was extremely dangerous. Four men were killed during its construction.

Greenfield was rocked by another death. Harry Greb's lifestyle caught up with him, and he died on the operating table at the age of 32. Gene Tunney was a pallbearer at his funeral. The procession from St. Philomena's Church to Calvary Cemetery lasted for hours because nearly 3,000 onlookers blocked the path. Boys stood atop tombstones to get a good view, while young women alternated between crying and asking Tunney to strike a pose for them.

Greenfield families now had access to modern conveniences. Telephones were more affordable, especially with a party line, and families who could afford one took calls for neighbors. More

During pioneer times, it became illegal to sell liquor to Indians. Traders skirted the law by hiding liquor for sale in slim bottles tucked into their boots, hence the term "bootlegging."

WHAT IS A PARTY LINE?

In your home, you may have two or more phones on the same line. A "party line" was very similar, but instead of sharing the line with someone in your house, you might share it with a neighbor or two across the street. The shared party line phone would ring in all three houses, with the phone company using a different ring for each home to alert the tenants that the call was for them: one house might have two short rings, another one long and one short ring, another two long rings. As phone systems became more sophisticated, the party line would ring only in the house to which the call was directed.

The Pittsburgh-McKeesport airport was later called Bettis Field after Lt. Cyrus Bettis, an air service pilot who died in a 1926 plane crash.

importantly, almost everyone in Greenfield had access to plumbing and filtered water. Still, most were working long hours under poor conditions and any disease could be fatal. Deaths from the flu in Pittsburgh numbered over 2,000, more people than were just killed in action during World War I.

Options opened for airplane pilots, and those who made their living barnstorming could now get commercial jobs. Pilots flew Pittsburgh newspapers to train stations each morning so travelers could read them as they rode the Pennsylvania Railroad to Pittsburgh. Airplanes were so plentiful that the county built a 40-acre commercial airport, Pittsburgh-McKeesport Field, to alleviate traffic in the smaller airports that had popped up in and around the city.

One morning, a bizarre sight awakened residents all over Greenfield and Hazelwood. Log crosses were on fire at Fort Black. Their placement at the fort, the most visible point in town, ensured that they could be seen a mile away—and they were. The Ku Klux Klan was announcing its presence in town.

The Ku Klux Klan began as a harmless Tennessee social club created by a half-dozen Confederate veterans. It changed to a vigilante group when Republican Reconstructionists in Tennessee extended voting and other rights to Blacks. Dressed like ghosts in white robes and white pointed masks, KKK members rode around at night on their horses. These scare rides metamorphosed into posses that beat and murdered Blacks and Republicans. Congress passed a Ku Klux Klan Act in 1871, and the federal interest stopped the KKK in its tracks.

Nearly 50 years later, William Joseph Simmons entered the picture. Simmons' father had been a member of the old KKK. Simmons himself was a great joiner and already belonged to at least half a dozen social clubs including the Odd Fellows and the Masons. He even made his living as a colonel from one of these organizations, Woodmen of the World.

The time was at the advent of motion pictures, one of the most popular of which was D.W. Griffith's *Birth of a Nation*. Its screenplay, based on a bestseller by Thomas Dixon, Jr. called *The Clansman*, showed the KKK as a noble organization saving the South from the threat of cruel, inhuman Blacks after the Civil War. The movie sold out 280 consecutive performances in New York City and ran for nearly a year. Protests and violence at theaters in the North only increased its popularity. It spurred Simmons to revive the Klan.

The old Klan no longer existed, so he created a new one from scratch. He wrote up the rules: members must be Protestant, they must be white, and they must be born in the United States. They must take an oath to support the following things:

- keep Anglo-Saxon American civilizations, institutions, politics and society pure
- prevent unwarranted strikes by foreign agitators
- advocate sensible and patriotic immigration laws
- maintain forever white supremacy in all things

A burning cross would be their symbol that "America is Protestant and so it must remain."

Simmons tried to get his new Klan off the ground, but he didn't have much success—that is, until he joined forces with two big-city advertising agents, Edward Young Clarke and Elizabeth Tyler. These two shifty characters had just gotten out of jail for disorderly conduct, and Clarke had once been arrested for carrying liquor immediately after he gave a speech complaining that Prohibition was not being enforced. Clarke, Tyler and Simmons had in common one driving force—the search for the angle, the pitch, the final scheme that would make them all rich.

They set up the KKK as a pyramid scheme. Clarke would be the Imperial Kleagle in charge of recruiting. They would charge a $10 initiation fee that they grandly called a Klectoken. Four dollars would go to the local Kleagle who recruited the member; $1 to the King Kleagle in charge of recruiting for that state; 50 cents to the regional recruiter, the Grand Goblin; $2.50 to Clarke and Tyler; and $2 to Simmons.

Clarke and Tyler worked an incredible door-to-door sales campaign waged on the very real fear that Catholic immigrants might take Protestant men's jobs. The team entered a town and approached its most prominent businesspeople, whom they told that to display "TWK" (code for Trade With Klansmen) in their windows would dramatically increase business. Even preachers were approached and told that, since the KKK put such an emphasis on Protestantism, membership in the KKK would increase church attendance. Before they left town, Clarke and Tyler would stage the highlight of their visit: an initiation ceremony under the light of torches and large, burning crosses.

Newspapers started to attack the Klan and what it stood for. Simmons was investigated by Congress, which had a surprising effect. Klan membership really took off, sometimes at a rate of 5,000 new members a day. In a little over a year, they had 85,000 new members, which meant $212,000 for Clarke and Tyler and $170,000 for Simmons—not including the $1 they made on every $6.50 costume. Though many of the members were law-abiding citizens taken in by Clarke and Tyler preying on their fears, the Klan took anyone, no matter how dangerous, as long as they were white, Protestant and had $10.

At this time, one of the country's most concentrated Catholic populations was in Allegheny County. Clarke and Tyler targeted the area, and soon Allegheny County had one of the heaviest Klan

Pennsylvania's King Kleagle, Sam D. Rich, had an office in downtown Pittsburgh's Jenkins Arcade.

One dollar in the time of Simmons' KKK was worth about $10 in the year 2000.

After they were accepted and had paid their "Klectoken," a Klansmen could later be banished for moral indiscretions, though those chastised didn't always take it seriously. At a Klan "trial" of a man who was charged with "living with a woman not his wife," the accused simply told his prosecutors to mind their own business.

populations in the United States, claiming 33 lodges throughout the county. One of these was the Victory Klan, right over the hill from Fort Black in neighboring Hazelwood.

Though the Klan also despised Blacks and Jews, their main target was Catholic immigrants. Klansmen were bold in the face of the law, even marching in the nation's capital. They kept a low profile, however, in towns like Greenfield, where they were greatly out-numbered by Catholics. Ten miles east in the town of Carnegie, a Klansman attending an outdoor speech by his Imperial Wizard was killed by an anti-Klan mob.

This heyday of the Klan didn't last long, and their fall came from within their own ranks. Pennsylvania Klansmen sued each other, revealing all the Klan secrets in the courts, including the fact that it was run entirely for profit. But the members of the Klan got what they wanted—steps toward a white Protestant America. Officially, all countries were issued an immigration limit, but the

TEXT FROM KLAN RECRUITMENT PAMPHLETS, CIRCA 1920s (MISSPELLINGS ARE THEIRS)

Ku Klux Klan Rides Again
Pro-Protestant, Christian, White Militant
Organization Believes We Should:

Register and Fingerprint all Aliens. Stop Immigration for Ten Years. Depart all Aliens and Undesriables. Banish from our Country every Foreign "Ism," Nazi Ism, Communism, Fascism. Protect the Public School. Keep AMERICA Protestant. "Put None But Americans On Guard." Do You Believe in Protestant, Christian America ? If so, Write P. O. Box 4565, Philadelphia, Pa.

FROM ANOTHER KLAN PAMPHLET, FRIENDLY DONT'S TO IMMIGRANTS

DON'T forget we have given you a haven. Respect our charity or go back.
DON'T attempt to change our form of government. We are satisfied with it. We made it through blood and we are quite ready to maintain it through blood. **Don't forget that!**
DON'T forget for one moment that citizenship is a great privilege—not an inherent right, and that it can be taken away as well as granted
DON'T forget that there are over one hundred million potential volcanoes in the United States. An American mob is not a pretty thing, but it is earnest and ruthless.
THIS IS AMERICANISM.

numbers tell the true story: Palestine's limit was 100, Italy's was 4,000, Russia's was 2,000. During the same year, Great Britain's limit was 34,000 and Germany's was 51,000. Asians were forbidden to immigrate at all.

Later in the same year that crosses lit the sky over Fort Black, the fort was torn down. ◆

During the first 20 years of the 20th century, Pittsburgh's Catholic Diocese bought or built a new building every month.

17 | A Walk Through Greenfield

No one, not even the KKK, was going to scare Greenfield's immigrants from their new homes. They were here to stay, working in the mills or setting up shops to serve the millworkers and their families. The Avenue became a bustling shopping district, with tiny delicatessens and candy stores scattered about the surrounding streets. Let's take an imaginary walk up Greenfield Avenue in this day and time. We'll start at the railroad trestle in The Run.

Now if you stand at the railroad trestle looking up Greenfield Avenue and turn to your right to head down Irvine Street, about a mile along, you would come to Hazelwood's bustling business district. We'd be heading there if we were getting ready for a holiday supper.

If we wanted something very, very special in the way of food, we went to Hazelwood where you could buy a live chicken. They would tie the legs together and put it on the scale—sometimes the darn thing fluttered off and landed down on the floor. You could take it home and kill it yourself, or you could have the butcher kill it. Then you poured boiling water over it so the feathers would come out easier.

But for everyday shopping, we'll head up the hill along Greenfield Avenue. There are shops and stores all along the way, and when you get to the top of the hill, the stretch of road where it levels off holds the main business district.

Right now, let's walk up The Avenue, starting our tour in The Run. On the left, across from the First Baptist Church, are Mr. Ponteri's barber shop, Dunay's drugstore and Doelfel's candy store. You might be surprised to know that Mr. Doelfel, who is blind, can always give you the right change.

Up a little farther is the Second Avenue Ten Cent Building and Loan, across the street from the B&O Railroad field office.

My mother and dad built a home, and I used to have to go down The Run to the building and loan to pay the mortgage.

Next to the building and loan is Mr. Kleppick's laundry and Carmen Milto's shoe repair shop. Across from that is the iceman and Liska's grocery.

A little farther up the hill is Twigg's jewelers and Yalch's drugstore. Cisar's candy store is next to Gratton's grocery.

Gratton's store took care of all Greenfield. They delivered. My mother got from them, and we lived up on Hazelwood Avenue. They came and took the order, and they would come back and deliver it.

On the right, along the way, we pass some row houses where the "colored" people live. Past the Swinburne Bridge is another small grocery run by Nicholas Hamas. Across the street is the real estate office and Raczka's shoe repair, and up from that is Hakim's clothing store. Then we see Cipa's grocery and up from that on the left is Lamberson's service station.

On your right, up Yoder Street are some small farms where people raise chickens and ducks, and there are even a few horses up there. Cross Yoder Street. Do you smell the ammonia? That's Austin's Market. They make cleaning solutions in the basement, then they bottle and sell them.

You've heard of Austin's Carpet Cleaner? They used to make that right here. The fumes would go all over Greenfield, you could smell it.

We used to go down to Austin's Market from school during Lent. They had a big barrel of dill pickles and we used to buy one for a nickel when we weren't eating candy during Lent.

Cross Kearcher Street to get to Cauley's candy store. Across the street are the steps to Greenfield School.

Up to the level part of The Avenue, and now we're out of The Run and up to the business district. On the left is St. Rosalia School and their beautiful church, built with contributions from parishioners who gave money to "buy a brick." Beautiful stained glass windows bear the names of the families who donated them.

School must have just let out because students are gathered around talking with the priests and nuns.

Father Lavelle was such a wonderful priest, he was so handsome. The girls would run over and grab his hand and Sister would get so angry. She'd say, "Don't you know that's the hand that serves the Eucharist? You're not allowed to touch a priest's hand."

St. Rosalia High School is restricted to girls only now. The diocese is concentrating its resources on the breadwinners, the boys, and they are attending the new Central Catholic High School in Oakland. The school is every bit as strict as St. Rosalia, but of course that doesn't stop the boys from loafing on St. Rosalia's school steps or hanging out outside McMillin's drugstore after school and on weekends. Father prefers they hang out in the lyceum where he can keep an eye on them.

You can be sure that later this evening, the nuns will be peeking out the window to see if any of their students are loafing on The Avenue. You can be equally sure that if they see any goings-on that Father Faughnan will address them in his sermon at Mass on Monday morning before school starts.

In front of St. Rosalia Church is a group of folks waiting for the streetcar. If you look behind the church, you can see the parish's three-floor lyceum. The basement of the lyceum has an auditorium where dances are held, and where schoolchildren and alumni put on plays. The auditorium's stage is also where the students take their tap dance lessons. The first floor has bowling alleys and pool tables. The janitor's apartment is in a corner of the second floor, alongside the gymnasium where St. Rosalia's girls' basketball team practices.

Continuing up The Avenue, on your right is Dr. McLenahan's office at the corner of Lydia Street.

> *Dr. McLenahan's office was where Kanai's is now. Where you go in the side to the funeral home, that's where you went into his office. He lived there and he had two sons and a daughter, I think. The youngest son became a doctor, and he delivered some of my babies.*

Across the street on the other corner is McMillin's drugstore. There's a soda fountain inside, and there are boys outside holding up the lamppost.

> *During Lent we didn't eat candy, and we went to the drugstore and bought horehound candy. It tastes like medicine so we figured it wasn't candy.*

Next door is Rudolph's meat market. Then comes another shoemaker, Rocco Minetti, and next to him Doelfel's has another candy store. Up near Coleman Street, on your right is Kirwan Flannery's funeral home.

Cross Coleman and on your left is another candy store, owned by Harry Daniels. Next to that is Dryden Brothers grocery. If it starts to rain, we can hide under their canopy—it reaches all the way out to the curb.

> *Dryden's, that was a grocery store. The couple who ran it never had children. They were both tall and thin, and kind of cranky. You could charge things. Dad used to go down on the weekend and pay the bill.*

Next is the Kroger grocery, which has a bakery, too. Past Kroger's is the Greenfield Theater, which used to show silent movies but now also runs the new "talkies."

Every Saturday we got a quarter. I think the show cost 15 cents. We would go to the show, then go in McMillin's and buy a sundae or a soda. It was a nice little show, it wasn't too big.

Then comes Hakim's dry goods store and the A&P grocery, and across from them is Dr. Ertzman's office.

I was born in our house on Gladstone Street. Dr. Ertzman come up with his little black bag, and the neighbor kids stood out in the front yard while he delivered me. I wonder if he ever got paid for it.

Cross Hoosac to get to Noren's dry goods.

Noren's Dry Goods Store. You could buy any kind of yard goods, needles, thread, yarn, knitting needles, anything like that, you know, dry goods.

An older couple had Noren's. That was a nice little store. I always liked embroidery and things like that, and we used to go down and buy little things like placemats and we'd sit and embroider. They had baby dresses, and you could buy little gifts down there.

On the other side of the street is Eyrings Bakery.

Right direct across from Noren's was a baker shop. We used to love for my mother to say we could go down to buy sweet rolls at lunch. We got a dozen sweet rolls and we were in our glory.

Up from that is Midge Laughlin's butcher shop. If you call and order meat, they'll deliver it, but neighborhood kids are always happy to walk down to pick up the order because Mr. Laughlin gives them pieces of wieners.

Then the Hub dry cleaner—they'll pick up and deliver your clothes.

Hub Cleaner. I worked with him on Saturdays, to bring the cleaning to the houses. What'd I make, a quarter a day, I forget. I didn't last too long, 'cause I'll tell you why. He used to fall asleep in the car, I'd go back down, he was sleeping, I'd have to wake him up. He was scary like. He was about four foot tall, he was a midget. He used to drive along and look at the wires. He scared me half to death. One day he fell asleep up on Windsor Street where we lived, he went right through somebody's front porch. Well, that woke him up.

Then another shoemaker, Pietro Christiano. Then Saul Cohen's place, a little grocery and deli where you can also get firecrackers and cigars.

Past Saul Cohen's, in the Cain apartment building, is Rimelin's Beauty Shoppe.

We used to go down to Rimelin's and get perms. They used to have to take your hair on heavy rods about four inches long. They rolled it, and your hair stood up straight in the air. Those things were hot and they were heavy. It was actually torture to have your hair done in those days.

Next door to Rimelin's is Cain's Market. If you turn to the right and look up Winterburn Street, you can see the Grote farm from where you are standing.

Cross the street to get to Chuck Prokopovitsh's Winterburn Pharmacy, where there's another soda fountain and another gang of boys on the corner. We can stop in for an ice cream cone with jimmies and a nickel soda pop, then head up The Avenue again. A few doors past the pharmacy is Dr. Archibald, the dentist. After that, except for Max Rosen's grocery, there is a straight stretch of homes ahead, many of them high up on the hill.

Schenley Park Bridge is on your left, down the hill a piece. Past the gas station you can see some folks walking out to the park to get a good seat in the grandstand for the sulky races tonight. If we were here earlier, we could have watched the men putting up the new

houses. Teachers have been complaining because their students are coming to school late because they stop to watch the construction.

Where The Avenue starts to bend, on your left is Magee Field. If you look down through the trees, you can see the new swimming pool.

As long as I can remember, they would not let colored people in the Greenfield pool. And of course there were colored people at the bottom of the hill in those days.

We have a few blocks to walk now, past the residential part of The Avenue. We will be clear past Windsor and Melbourne streets before you can see Roosevelt School.

When my daughter was going to be born, we moved up on Windsor Street, and of course that was too far to come down to Greenfield shopping. At that time, we had nice stores here at this end.

Roosevelt School, which goes up to the eighth grade, is the building on your left. Their playground faces Murray Avenue. Across the street is the Blank Confectionery. Cross Loretta Street and you'll see Barbara Yetter's grocery store. Past that is Bruno Buccina's shoe repair. Cross Montclair Street to get to the Church of the Brethren. They're selling this building to the Community Church of God. Mary

Albiez, the dressmaker, is up this way. Past Exeter Street is another A&P, Strauss Meat Market and another Kroger's.

In those days, the supermarkets had cookies in big bins covered with glass, and when you'd buy a pound they'd lift the glass and measure them out for you. When my little brother was about three years old, he ran away and got all the way down to the A&P. Somehow he got the lid open to the cookie bin and they found him down there, eating Lorna Doones.

If you walk all the way down to where The Avenue ends, you'll hit Hazelwood Avenue. You can make a right and walk down the hill to get to Gladstone School, and past that to the Hazelwood Library on Monongahela Street. It's a beautiful place and it even has an auditorium in the basement.

The library was always in Hazelwood, we never had a library over here. We had lots of saloons.

If you look up Bigelow Street, all along there, clear down to Flowers Avenue in Hazelwood, is where the farm owned by the Farmer family used to be. George Kaye Road was named after one of them and so was Flowers Avenue. Annie Flowers, a cousin of Stephen Collins Foster, is an old woman now and lives in a big old house on George Kaye Road. Everybody in town knows her—she's hard to miss.

Annie Flowers was something else. She never married and she was very stern. When she wanted something, she got it. If she wanted a ride somewhere, she'd get out right in the middle of the street and flap that big old black umbrella of hers, and people had to either stop or run her over. Then she'd give them a quarter and they'd take her home.

Make a left at Hazelwood Avenue and we'll go out to Murray Avenue, which runs parallel to Greenfield Avenue. There are shops along here, too, including Mr. Tambouri's grocery and restaurant. Near the big Morrowfield apartment building is the little deli and candy store Mr. and Mrs. Poli own. Around the corner on Forward Avenue is a little hot dog shop where the high school kids stop on their way home from Allderdice. That is, the kids who can afford a hot dog. ♦

The Community Church of God began in downtown Pittsburgh with preachers who traveled by riverboat holding revivals. The congregation had various homes in Greenfield before it moved to its current church, where it has been for more than half a century.

When the Stephen Foster Memorial was built, Annie Flowers donated the melodeon her cousin had played at her home.

18 | GOOD TIMES IN HARD TIMES

At one time, one-sixth of the glass used in the United States was made in or around Pittsburgh. In a single year, Pittsburgh Plate Glass, American Window Glass, United States Glass and other local factories produced 27 million square feet of plate glass, 175 million square feet of window glass, and 260 million bottles and jars.

Catholic orphans were placed in either St. Paul's Roman Catholic Orphan Asylum of Pittsburgh or in St. Joseph's Protectory. St. Paul's orphanage later merged with Holy Family Institute.

Times were now getting tough all over the country. In one single year, the number of Americans who were unemployed doubled. Pittsburgh, a city filled to the brim with busy factories and banks to handle their payrolls, had been a hotbed of prosperity. Now one by one banks were closing. Glass factories were slowing down and letting workers go. Steel production was at a low point.

Most families in Greenfield were used to hardship. When the Depression hit Pittsburgh, people just pulled up their bootstraps and dealt with it.

When we were married, I wore a dress of cornflower blue velvet with a high scooped neck and big puffed sleeves and a hat to match. I cut the bottom off and got a lot of use out of that dress, because I could wear it in the street. A lady down The Run used to sew and she made me a purse from the bottom of the dress.

Two or more families shared a house, each family taking a floor and sharing the kitchen and bathroom, which—you may remember—was often in the basement. Families took in foster children for the extra income it would provide.

People took in foster kids all over the place. Orphans, too. They'd bring them into their house and be paid to keep them there. And the kids would do the work. Some of them worked their little butts off.

Orphans and foster kids were discriminated against. They played with all the other kids, but after school they worked with the C-Y-something and cleaned the blackboards and polished the desks, and they got so much money for doing the work. There were a lot of them at St. Rosalia.

Every scrap of food was used, and leftovers became soup for tomorrow's supper. Bacon grease was spread on bread like butter, and when it got rancid, it was used as shoe polish. New clothing was often an unaffordable luxury, so women cut, sewed and reshaped their dresses and hats.

An overwhelming majority of Americans lost their faith in the Republican Party during the Depression and chose a Democratic president, Franklin Delano Roosevelt, to lead the country back to prosperity. In Pittsburgh, most voters even changed their political party to officially become Democrats. The following November, they were part of the highest off-year election voter turnout in Pennsylvania's history because two propositions on the ballot touched topics near and dear to their hearts—sports and booze.

The first referendum called for Pennsylvania to rewrite its "blue laws" to allow each city to choose whether the ban on Sunday toil applied to athletes. An affirmative vote would mean that each city could make its own interpretation of how the law applied to professional sports. There was no question in anyone's mind how Pittsburgh would vote. Even before the referendum was passed, the city's police superintendent was in the stands cheering on the Pirates, the new pro football team.

The second vote, even more important, was whether the United States should just give it up and let go of Prohibition. The 18th Amendment was easily repealed, and the commonwealth of Pennsylvania took over the liquor business, opening "state stores" run by its Liquor Control Board. Taverns started to replace some of the stores on Greenfield Avenue.

Pittsburgh politics was no longer run by the old Magee-Flinn ring, but the city had a new mayor who did his best to keep the old controversy alive. His first day on the job, Mayor William McNair had his desk moved to the lobby of his building "so the people can reach me." He moved it from the cold hallway to a warm office a few days later. Once he had an orchestra set up in the hallway to play while he did his paperwork. His short career as mayor was topped off by a week's stage engagement playing the fiddle, a ride on a steer through the downtown streets and two incarcerations— one for refusing to refund a $100 fine that had been collected wrongly and the second for misbehavior.

Programs to provide food and medical care for children, the widowed and the elderly were already well established in other countries. Britain had passed a Social Security Act almost 20 years before the Depression began. Even third-world countries like Uruguay and Chile had social security programs ten years before the United States did. Now, with President Roosevelt at the helm, the United States finally passed a Social Security Act.

My dad dropped dead at 52 years old and left my mother with nine children, so it was kind of rough, but thank God for Social Security because we lived on that.

The government also provided badly needed work for young men by creating the CCC and the WPA.

As the Depression receded, much needed construction began in every corner of the city. Streets that were adequate when the immigrants arrived now carried a lot more traffic and were in need of repair. Workers leveled roads to make them easier to travel, and most of the city's streets were paved. A new airport, 400 acres larger

Since 1932, seats on Pittsburgh's City Council have been held exclusively by Democrats.

The Pittsburgh Pirates football team changed their name in 1940 to the Pittsburgh Steelers.

WHAT WERE THE CCC AND THE WPA?

The **Civilian Conservation Corps** was a volunteer army of construction workers. Young men 17 to 27 years of age signed up for nine-month terms during which they worked for the CCC in national parks and other federal land improvements.

The **Works Progress Administration** hired workers to improve transportation, building highways, airports and bridges. They also hired thousands of writers and artists to work on various cultural projects. Over the eight years it existed, the WPA employed 8.5 million people in the United States.

than the old one, was built in West Mifflin and christened the Allegheny County Airport.

Atlantic City was the vacation spot of choice for those who could afford a trip to the seashore. Greenfield Jimmy Smith frequently took his family to this popular resort where they would hobnob with the rich and famous.

One fateful day, Jimmy ran into prizefighter Billy Conn and introduced him to his 15-year-old daughter, Mary Louise. When Billy asked Jimmy for permission to take Mary Louise to dinner that night, since Billy was so much older—he was 20—Jimmy readily agreed. It would be a nice treat for his little girl, he thought, something she would remember. She would remember, all right. At

dinner, Billy announced, "I'm going to marry you." Mary Louise laughed him off, but Billy was serious, and that night their courtship began.

Greenfield Jimmy was beside himself. He hoped for his daughter to marry someone with class and breeding, not an "uneducated pug" from East Liberty.

Greenfield Jimmy didn't like Billy Conn dating his daughter. I can remember Billy coming down to visit her in his convertible right on The Avenue there, and kids would be all around the car. One day, Greenfield Jimmy chased him down Winterburn Street. They said that if Greenfield Jimmy Smith and Billy Conn ever really went at it, Billy would have lost. Probably because of the way Jimmy fought—he wasn't that big. Jimmy, he was a street fighter, a bar fighter.

Greenfield Jimmy found a cloistered school for Mary Louise— Philadelphia's Rosemont, where she would be under the Sisters' watchful eye. When he delivered his daughter to their door, he gave firm instructions she was never to see a Mr. Billy Conn. But Billy was persistent. He deluged her with letters and presents, and won her heart.

When Mary Louise finally became of legal age, she and Billy drove north of Pittsburgh and applied for a marriage license. They

WHO WAS BILLY CONN?

William David Conn, Jr. was born and raised in the East Liberty section of Pittsburgh. He fought his first professional bout when he was 16 years old. (He was beat in four rounds and walked away with a purse of $2.50. His manager gave him 50 cents.) Conn's career lasted 13 years and 75 bouts: 63 wins, 11 losses, 1 draw. At one point, he had a streak of 27 straight wins.

Conn was a handsome man and extremely popular. When he fought at the Duquesne Gardens, extra streetcars were needed because of the enormous crowds.

Billy Conn was the light-heavyweight champion of the world for three years running until he decided to fight Joe Louis for the heavyweight title. Conn was far ahead of Louis on points when, against the advice of his manager, Billy went after his opponent for a knockout. Louis knocked Billy cold with two seconds left in the 13th round.

Billy Conn and Joe Louis fought two rematches after the war was over. In the first, Billy was knocked out in the 8th round. The second he lost on decision.

Billy Conn retired when he was 27 years old.

To be married in the Roman Catholic Church, couples are required to "post the banns" to ensure that there are no impediments to their marriage. A parish priest announces the impending marriage from the pulpit for three consecutive weeks, after which the couple may be wed.

hoped, like most Catholics, to be married by the bride's pastor and posted their banns at St. Philomena's Catholic Church in Squirrel Hill. When Greenfield Jimmy found out, he went straight to the bishop and warned him to stop the wedding.

Billy Conn and his beautiful girlfriend couldn't get married here in Pittsburgh 'cause Greenfield Jimmy called the bishop, told him, "Stop this wedding. No pug fighter's marrying my beautiful educated daughter."

Undaunted, Billy and Mary Louise drove east. While Greenfield Jimmy was sending the state police after them, the young couple found a kindly priest in Philadelphia who performed a quiet wedding. By the time anyone caught up with them, they were already on their honeymoon.

Folks didn't have to travel to Atlantic City for entertainment. It was right in their own backyard.

About eight of us girls took a walk every night after supper, after we washed the dishes. We went up Greenfield Avenue, through the park toward Oakland and down the winding road, Swinburne, to home. Every night, and twice on Sundays. And it wasn't so much the walking, but we met boys up where the merry-go-round used to be. We met different boys over on the other side of Oakland, too, around the bandstand.

Couples danced in church basements and social halls. Dances were held on the tennis court at Magee Field, illuminated by strings of lights tied to the top of the fence. Mr. Collins' brickyard was no longer operating, and its horse barn was now the Glory Barn, a popular dance hall and bingo parlor. There were dances at the trolley barn in Hazelwood and at the Baptist church on Hazelwood Avenue near Brown's Hill. Young folks took the streetcar to Kennywood where they could swim all day, grab a quick dinner at the cafeteria and then dance late into the evening. North of the city, just two streetcars away, was another dance hall at West View Park. Families attended free Sunday concerts at the bandstand near the Oval in Schenley Park. Now that the "blue laws" had relaxed enough to exclude motion pictures, even on a Sunday the Park Theater was packed with folks watching the double feature, cartoons and newsreels.

A nickel in a child's pocket often meant an afternoon's walk to "the big Isaly's," the beautiful white Isaly ice cream factory on the Boulevard of the Allies in Oakland. The nickel bought one of their trademark skyscraper cones. The soda jerk would dip into round bins of fresh ice cream with a long oval scoop to create a cone six inches tall. If it was someone's birthday and a child was sent to bring home a special treat, the white-garbed Isaly workers plopped it into a bag full of dry ice so it would stay cold throughout the long walk home.

My mother used to send me over to the big Isaly's for one quart of hand-packed vanilla. And I'd get a strawberry milkshake. They used Isaly's ice cream and real strawberries and handed you that cold shaker. It was delicious.

And if there was no nickel to spend? Boys fished, swam in the river or built forts in the woods.

We used to swim in the river, we shouldn't have done. We skinny-dipped. I once saw a big log floating down and tried to cross the river with it. I got off the log to stand and sunk into some kind of muck up to my armpits. Grease, or whatever, was emanating from the mill. I thought I was going to be sucked under. Never did anything like that again.

We were forbidden to swim in the rivers. My dad forbid us. 'Cause when we come out, we'd be smellin' like fish.

Groups of kids bowled or played basketball in St. Rosalia's lyceum. Young folks roller-skated and took long walks to Hazelwood or Homestead to stroll past the movie theaters and look in the shop windows.

The High Level Bridge hadn't been opened yet. It was blocked off at both ends but it looked finished. That was our private roller-skating rink. It was spectacular. We were warned not to be on there, but who cared?

Dry ice is solid carbon dioxide. In the days when folks traveled by streetcar, stores that sold perishables often packed their products in dry ice so they would stay cold until the customer got home.

The year of the big flood, Father Faughnan passed away, and Father Matthew Coughlan took over St. Rosalia parish. Father Coughlan had his hand in every pie, presiding over every baptism, wedding and funeral in the parish, leaving little work for the younger priests who assisted him. He had a seat built for himself in the schoolyard, on a round black railing surrounding the sycamore tree. Students quickly learned to say a respectful "hello" as he sat there after school, smoking his Fatima cigarettes and keeping an eye on the children as they made their way home.

> Just as you come out of the church to the alleyway, there was the biggest, fattest sycamore tree, and Father had a bench built around it. He sat there and watched the kids coming out of school, frightened them to death, of course.

> Now St. Rosalia's the only church in this whole world where the collection for Mass is taken from the back to the front, and I heard that began during Father Coughlan's reign. I think he suspected that by the time the collection got to the back of the church the ushers were pocketing some of the money. So collecting from back to front and putting the money on the altar, it was his.

The Billy Conn-Joe Louis fight for the heavyweight crown was the biggest event to hit Greenfield for a long time. Folks crowded into each other's living rooms to drink cold beers while the children played board games, and waited for the fight to be broadcast on the radio or television. Out at Forbes Field, the baseball game was halted while a blow-by-blow description of the fight boomed over the Pittsburgh Pirates' sound system. Around the United States, an estimated 150,000 people watched the Billy Conn-Joe Louis championship fight on one of the country's 5,000 TV sets. This meant an average of 30 people in front of each set, many of whom were watching television for the very first time.

Billy Conn wasn't the only casualty that year. Schenley Park's beloved merry-go-round sat idle during the Depression and was victim to the elements and to scavengers.

> The enormous round carousel in Schenley Park, it was a beautiful thing to behold. When it was in disrepair and about to be torn down, we all stole bits of it. Had those for years, handworked horses and things like that.

The city sold what was left of the gorgeous carousel to a wrecking company for $23.50. ◆

On St. Patrick's Day in 1936, downtown rivers rose to a crest of 46 feet. The National Guard was called in, and homes in Squirrel Hill and Greenfield were without water or electricity for two days.

Kennywood built its Noah's Ark funhouse the same year as the St. Patrick's Day flood.

19 THE HOME FRONT

December 7. My brother, his friend and I had gone to the show to see "Sun Valley Serenade" with John Payne and Sonja Henie. Afterward we walked down by the Grill. There were these guys standing outside—at the time, I thought they were older but they were probably in their 20s—and they proceeded to tell us that the Japanese had bombed Pearl Harbor. The whole avenue, the whole picture of that day still sticks in my mind.

Before an official declaration of war, Greenfield's men were already involved in the European conflict: they worked at the steel mills that supplied America's allies with much needed tools and weapons. The involvement became official when the Pearl Harbor Naval Base in Hawaii was hit in a surprise attack by 353 Japanese bomber planes. President Roosevelt declared war against Japan and the United States joined its European allies in World War II.

Young men in Greenfield enlisted, or were drafted, to serve their country.

I was a telephone lineman in the field artillery, strung wire from the main headquarters to the firing battalions so the commanders could get firing orders back and forth. Artillery fire is always scary because you can't do anything about it, they're just blowing holes all around you. Being 18 years old, you didn't really know any better. You need young men there, people who do things before they think about them. You're better off if you don't think about it too much.

Skilled millhunks who would be hard to replace were given deferments and did their part for the war effort by keeping the tools and weapons coming. Women worked in factory and mill jobs vacated by men off at war. Patriotic youngsters were eager participants in scrap drives, collecting tin cans, bacon grease and newspapers for the war effort—though most kids were never quite sure how these items actually helped the government and held secret suspicions that the purpose of the scrap drive was to keep them busy and feeling useful.

The federal government issued ration coupons, and people did without meat, sugar, gasoline and shoes for the sake of the war effort. Sugar and butter were in short supply, and there was always a rush to the lucky store that got the latest shipment. News passed through the neighborhood that a grocer in Greenfield or Squirrel Hill had sugar, and schoolchildren were sent off hurriedly after school clutching money and ration coupons.

American men between the ages of 18 to 45 were drafted into military service during World War II.

Like all the other theater owners in the country, the owner of the Park Theater on The Avenue showed patriotic newsreels between his double features. A softhearted gent, he pretended that the 13- and 14-year-olds who *swore* they were under 12, *really*, had him fooled and let them in for half price. The theater was so full on a Saturday afternoon that children had to step over friends sitting in the aisles to get to their seats. They ate popcorn, threw candy at each other and stayed all afternoon.

Down the street a few blocks was Mary Burns' saloon. When McMillin's Drug Store moved a block up The Avenue, the Greenfield Grill took over the corner of Greenfield Avenue and Lydia Street. The Grill was owned by a neighborhood widow named Mary Burns Vogel. As in most towns, local ordinances forbade a tavern next door to a church and school, but St. Rosalia's Father Coughlan obtained a waiver for Mary.

Mary promised to run a respectable place, and she did. She made sure that men were "shut off" when they had too much to drink and banned them from the bar for six months if they balked.

You'd see this on The Avenue many times. Somebody'd say, "Let's go down to Mary's and get a beer." Somebody else'd say, "I'm not allowed. She won't let me in." She wouldn't. She would remember.

She was a good cook, and families had dinner at her tavern. On Fridays, her block on The Avenue was a busy place as men stopped on the way home from work for fish sandwiches to take home from Rudolph's Market or deviled crabs from the Greenfield Grill. Of course, the millhunks usually had to stop at the Frankstown Club and the Soldiers and Sailors—or Tam's, if they were at the top of The Avenue—before they got there. Just to say hello, of course.

Greenfielders were still a mixed lot, and you could find a stripper from one of the downtown bars living next door to a neighborhood cop. Schoolchildren all knew each other. Whether due to the close proximity of the houses or the nature of the people, it was a tight community. More and more of the well-to-do Protestant families had moved away over the years, and the town was now a mill town and overwhelmingly Catholic. There wasn't a lot of "keeping up with the Joneses" because the Joneses weren't doing any better than anybody else. Going out to dinner for a millhunk's family meant fish sandwiches at one of the neighborhood taverns or burgers and fries at the diner car at the top of Brown's Hill.

Never saw any displays of wealth in Greenfield, I don't think anybody was rich. I don't remember any ostentation of any kind.

There were few farms left, though at the top of the hill near Bigelow Street, there were folks who kept pigeon coops, and one family even had a black and white horse named Lightning that neighborhood kids loved to visit. There was still a farm between Haldane and Kearcher streets but its land was now simply a meadow. The enormous farmhouse with its great big windows that curved at the top and its ballroom and formal dining room was now the home of elderly sisters, one of whom mowed the entire pasture herself without a tractor. Since there were no fences between the yards, the meadow was a sled-riding delight in the wintertime, kids speeding on their Flexible Flyers from Stanley Street clear to the yards on Haldane. Another farm on Winterburn Street across from the fire house had its meadow appropriated by neighborhood kids for a ballfield. The Grotes no longer grazed cows in the valley that was now McCaslin Street. Instead, Greenfield's high schoolers drove their parents' cars a little too fast down the hill on the newly paved road.

WHAT WAS THE G.I. BILL?

As early as the Revolutionary War, veterans received benefits of one type or another, whether it was "mustering out" pay, land grants or pensions for the disabled. During World War II, President Franklin D. Roosevelt signed what is commonly known as the "G.I. Bill of Rights," which provided education and training, loan guaranty to buy a home, farm or business, and unemployment pay of up to $20/week. Two million veterans went to college after the war, and more than 3 million more went to trade schools.

In Greenfield, everyone started high school but not everyone finished it. Boys got work in the mills as soon as they were old enough, though many families encouraged at least the oldest boy to graduate from high school. With the war over, some returning Greenfield men were ambitious enough to attempt college under the G.I. Bill. Meanwhile, packs of Catholic boys took the streetcar to Central Catholic High School in Oakland every day or walked to school through The Run and along the railroad tracks. Central was a ticket out of the mill for a boy who dreamed of a white-collar job. Lawyers, priests, politicians, heart surgeons all escaped the mill under the tutoring of the Christian Brothers. Pittsburgh was building an "old-boy" network in which a Central ring on a young man's hand at a job interview could mean the start of a great career.

The Central boys suspected that Taylor Allderdice students had parties all day long. A co-ed school? How could you get an education there? Central was as far removed from a party as anyone could imagine. Boys wore suit jackets at all times, and removal of a tie meant detention. Lunch was monitored to make sure there were no fights, food or otherwise. Afterward the boys were led to the quadrangle behind the school to walk off their aggressiveness, parading continuously under the scrutiny of the vice principal. If a boy so much as giggled, it meant detention. Central boys learned a respect for authority, whether they wanted it or not.

> *Central was strict, very strict. You did do what you were told and you didn't argue about it. Anybody who hesitated wished they hadn't.*

> *The Christian Brothers are known for their discipline. Anything in their classroom that discombobulated their aura of sanctity and quiet and dignity was not just frowned on but dealt with. They would pick you up out of your chair and fling you against the blackboard just to get your attention.*

Meanwhile, Noren's Dry Goods sold neckties for the high school girls at St. Rosalia—red for freshmen, yellow for sophomores, blue for juniors and green for seniors. This tracking system helped the nuns keep their charges in line, and they had their work cut out for them. Girls taking typing class in the lyceum sneaked through the tunnel underneath and out the pastor's garage door. They crept into the principal's office to call the police or the fire department. The Sisters gave the older girls jodhpurs and boots and walked them to the stables at Schenley Park to work off their "high-spiritedness" by horseback riding. The girls rode their horses through the cinder trails that wound through the park, down to Panther Hollow and all around it—looking for boys, of course. The bold attitude of St. Rosalia's girls did come in handy on the basketball court—the team was known for its aggressiveness.

In the evenings, of course, the Central boys and the St. Rosalia girls got together. Weekends often meant sandlot football with the Montclair Ramblers or the Greenfield Preps playing teams like Art Rooney's North Side Civics.

> *We played a team from Squirrel Hill one day and a fight broke out. They won the game but we won the fight, and we figured that was a good day.*

Dates were usually a streetcar ride to a movie and to Reymer's downtown, or a walk to a show in Hazelwood or Homestead.

Couples walked arm in arm to Kelly's Barbecue or the Hot Puppie on Forward Avenue. Long walks were a form of entertainment in themselves. Young people held hands in the evening and strolled to the top of one of the hills in Greenfield with a view of downtown to check the Gulf Building for tomorrow's weather.

We used to walk out Second Avenue, over the Glenwood Bridge, up through Hays to the High Level Bridge, and over the High Level Bridge and up and down Hazelwood Avenue. Just to go for a walk.

High schoolers held parties at each others' houses or got together and rented the Soldiers and Sailors Hall near Magee Field. The more adventurous gathered up at the Fort to build bonfires, roast marshmallows and drink Virginia Dare wine. If a boy was able to borrow a car, it was a sure bet that a date would end at the slag dumps or Schenley Oval.

Everybody used to go over to the slag dump. That was quite a sight to behold. Rows and rows of slag cars came up along the top—they'd ride a little railroad car underneath. They used to pull them along the top, then dump them over and molten steel would pour down the side. Just like volcanic lava or something. Hot and red. Wild, I mean it'd light up the whole sky. So in between necking you'd look at it.

A group of young adults who had attended St. Rosalia and Central formed their own theater group, The Parish Players. Their first play, "Life With Father," was an attempt to raise money for basketball uniforms for the girls' basketball team. St. Rosalia's Sister Ann chose the plays and even gave the enthusiastic actors money for expensive trimmings like flocked wallpaper for the sets.

Because it was "Life With Father" we all had to have red hair. Two of the boys had natural red hair, but the rest of us didn't and we were disinclined to dye our hair flaming red. So I found some makeup downtown, a cake mascara that if you wet it and put it on a toothbrush it would dry to a bright red under the lights. It was like cardboard when it dried, and if anybody in the cast happened to touch each other or pat each other on the back, a cloud of red dust would rise up.

"Life With Father" was a great success and other plays soon followed. Neighbors scratched their heads in wonder as they watched these eager thespians carry a couch down Kearcher Street or a coat rack along The Avenue, all headed for the lyceum and the theater set. They worked long hours on these plays, building their own sets, making costumes from cast-off clothes and digging through basements and attics for the perfect wig or the right buttons. The plays became so popular that the theater troupe outgrew St. Rosalia's lyceum and performed in the larger auditorium at Greenfield School.

Afternoons found every street with a baseball game in progress. Every evening was filled with pickup games of Freeze Tag, Hide and Go Seek, Buck Buck and Release the Den.

We used to play out in the street in the evening. Lot of games—what the hell is that one? Buck Buck, how many fingers up. Goofy damn thing. We played it up against the walls in front of people's houses.

Kids had the run of the neighborhood, or thought they did. Many a boy was surprised to learn that his mother knew about the fight he was in an hour ago and three blocks away.

While these children were playing, sociologists all over the United States were publishing papers dissecting the behavior of their older brothers and sisters. If America's "melting pot" of immigrants kept their traditions, would that mean that social change was impossible for them? Would they never be assimilated into American culture? More importantly, would the gap between their lives and the lives of "real" Americans lead these adolescents to deviant behavior? ♦

In Buck Buck, one boy would bend over with his hands against a wall while his friends got in line. The first boy in line ran and jumped on the boy's back, then each boy in turn did the same until there was a huge pile of kids.

TVs, JDs and DAs

Financially, American families were better off after the Second World War than they had ever been. Parents who quit school in eighth grade to go to work were now sending their own children to high school. Adulthood was postponed at least until a child was 16. Working-class young people had leisure time. You could hear the grandmothers murmur, "Idle hands are the devil's workshop."

Americans had traditionally been permissive with their children. They had to be—they were too busy working to pay much attention to them. But during the decade when the parents of post-war teens were raised, the pendulum had shifted for a brief period of time, and for the first time the country was full of parents who were raised with an iron hand.

The short-lived trend of being strict with your children was ended by a pediatrician named Dr. Benjamin Spock. Though not totally against discipline, Dr. Spock favored the traditional American attitude of permissiveness. Moreover, his bestseller "Common Sense Book of Baby and Child Care" strongly suggested that, except in rare circumstances, mothers should devote themselves entirely and full time to caring for their children. Women read this to imply that if a child turned out bad, the mother was to blame.

Parents used Dr. Spock's book as a child-rearing bible, attempting to raise their offspring in this "modern" way but still expecting these children to be respectful, considerate, responsible—to act the way they had when they were brought up under the strict hand of their own parents. By comparison, their own children seemed wild, out of control.

Youngsters aged 13 to 19 were now considered a separate social group: teenagers. Sociologists had a field day studying them. Immigrants had not actually been assimilated into American culture, they said. There were too many gaps between the "haves" and the "have-nots," they said, though in Greenfield this gap had existed since John Turner's time. Cultural anthropologists insisted that it was natural for these have-not teens, denied access to upward mobility, to adopt what they termed "deviant behavior."

Deviant or nonconformist behavior, in their opinion, could only be a result of insanity. Scores of movies and television shows were made on the subject. Teenagers were seen as having a collective mental illness, and with the "baby boom" after World War II, there were more children and teens than ever before. All 48 states now had juvenile courts, and experts predicted that there would be one million "delinquent" teens by the middle of the decade. By their definition of delinquency, that number would actually be surpassed.

Society, alarmed at this new youth culture, created fantasy purity on TV. On television there were only two kinds of teens: good and bad. The separation was, for the most part, drawn along the line of wealth, with the good having money and the bad having none. Television and magazine advertisements showed women washing their floors in dresses and pearls, their families living lifestyles beyond the reach of most millhunks in Greenfield. The occasional "good but poor" television character was often portrayed in the patronizing way that a "good Negro" might be.

Greenfield's working-class families came from poor immigrant parents who had eked out a living in the mills. They weren't ashamed of their heritage. Rather, they were proud of the lessons it had taught them: hard work, ingenuity, responsibility, maturity at a young age. For the first time, now, these families who had worked so hard could afford a luxury like an evening watching television. But when they turned on the television set, they saw families like their own portrayed as bad, wrong or just plain laughable. Normal families, apparently, could afford to give their teenagers allowances so they could spend their afternoons dancing to the latest records and gossiping at the neighborhood soda fountain. Meanwhile, the teens in Greenfield's families were busy delivering groceries or ironing their younger siblings' clothes.

Television parents were well-to-do. The husband had a job that got him home every evening for a five-o'clock dinner with his family, where his wife, her hair coiffed in the latest style, would set a roast on the table when it wasn't even Sunday. A television mother didn't spend her day in the cellar putting bedspreads through the wringer washer while her husband was trying to get some sleep before his midnight shift at the mill. Television parents had conversations with their two children in the evening. The six or seven offspring of Greenfield's mothers and fathers were more likely to get their conversation from friends than from their busy parents. And often that conversation took place away from home, on the playground, on a walk around the block or in front of the corner store. Television was nothing like life in Greenfield.

A Greenfield boy, like the boys he saw on television, planned to work in the same profession as his father. However, his father didn't have a diaphanous job that disappeared at five o'clock. His father didn't walk through the front door after work in a suit. He came in through the cellar, taking off his dirty clothes before he walked into the house. Greenfield boys would get a job in the mill when they were old enough. It was hard work but it was steady, and folks expected to work hard. Most Greenfield boys weren't interested in

In a DA (duck's ass) haircut, a boy's hair was combed back on each side and then the hair in the back was combed flat on top. The result resembled a duck's tail.

During this time, 100 million comic books were sold monthly in the United States.

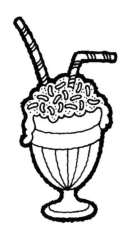

raising themselves to a higher social class, but in being able to hold on to the one they had.

Men and women were judged by different standards at this time, so it should come as no surprise that deviant behavior was judged differently for boys and girls. A "juvenile delinquent" boy hung on the corner in a street gang, terrorizing "good" kids and generally creating mayhem by fighting, stealing or vandalizing property. A girl was considered delinquent simply by keeping company with one of these boys.

The stigma attached to a girl losing her chastity was suddenly so great that, for the first time in the United States, almost half the new brides were teenagers.

We married young. No living together, that was a big sin. Folks were ostracized if there was anything like that. We got married.

A poor girl who had sex with a boyfriend might be sent to reform school; a rich girl who did the same might be committed to a mental institution.

It was easy for adults to spot these nonconformist juvenile delinquents. The boys wore tight blue jeans and slicked their hair back with pomade, a D.A. in the back and a wave or pompadour in the front. The girls on the corner wore bright Tangee lipstick, black eyeliner and tall, tall teased hair. Whatever money these teens had was spent on trappings of the new teen culture: comic books (adventure stories for the boys and romances for the girls), lipstick and hair pomade, and rock 'n' roll records.

The family Victrola was commandeered by teenagers no longer satisfied with their parents' Perry Como records. Portable transistor radios gave teens the opportunity to hear forbidden music without their parents' knowledge. They listened to outrageous singers like Elvis Presley or to "race music": rock 'n' roll sung by black artists and broadcast on Homestead radio stations WHOD or WAMO by their favorite disc jockey, Porky Chedwick, the "Daddio of the Raddio."

"Good" teenagers, on the other hand, congregated at a soda fountain rather than on a street corner. They dressed in fashionable styles considered suitable for a boy or girl of his or her age. Girls might wear a little pink lipstick on date night; boys would borrow their father's car and be sure to open the door for their date. In other words, the "right" kind of teenagers came from families who could afford to provide them with new clothes, cars and weekly allowances.

Parents were constantly on the lookout for "deviant behavior" in their children. The same experimentation that was once attributed to the natural exuberance of youth was now looked upon as a worrisome problem that needed to be corrected. Thirty-seven percent of Pittsburgh's children were already in strict parochial schools, and that number was even higher in places like Greenfield, with its large Catholic immigrant population. But even the firm hand of the nuns could not always repress these kids, and parents fretted on how to make their children behave and conform.

When my brother was in fifth grade, he was mischief. If the classroom window was open, he'd jump out the window. If Sister put us in a line to go to Stations of the Cross, he'd stand at the end of the line and duck it.

My brother and his friends used to bring cigars to school. They'd choke 'em, put them back in their pockets; you could still smell the smoke. Fourth grade!

Delinquency was frightening parents all over the country, though nearly half the juvenile offenses were not major crimes but minor infractions like truancy, disobeying parental or school authorities, or running away. Some sociologists insisted that the problem arose because immigrant groups were having a hard time adjusting to the American culture. A study by the National Invitational Conference on the Prevention and Control of Delinquency announced their conclusion that delinquency and lower-class behavior were one and the same. But though the worst juvenile

1957 TEEN ARRESTS IN PITTSBURGH

Crime	Number of Arrests	Percent Committed by Teens
Murder	2	8.0%
Robbery	80	22.3%
Burglary	367	39.9%
Larceny	359	47.9%
Auto theft	286	67.9%

offenders were assumed to come from the poorest families, in actuality most of the nation's young car thieves came from families with a little bit of money and were stealing cars for "kicks."

Teen crime was blamed not on the child, but on the parents. J. Edgar Hoover, head of the Federal Bureau of Investigation, announced that the outbreak of juvenile delinquency was due to a lack of both family discipline and religious training. President Dwight D. Eisenhower added the words "under God" to the Pledge of Allegiance that children recited before school each day. Bishop Fulton J. Sheen agreed with these assessments. Parents who were permissive and gave in to their children's demands raised children who would constantly seek new thrills or kicks. Parents who fought made children disdain all law. Parents who drank raised children with a penchant for violence. Parents were to blame. Society itself was blameless.

Some sociologists saw delinquency as normal, something that would be found in any modern city. They studied the culture of gang and corner life. On the corner, stealing would bring a boy glory and the respect of his peers. Being malicious—perhaps by terrorizing good children so they would be afraid to use the playgrounds and gyms where the gang congregated—would bring him status. Being wrong in the eyes of the law would bring him satisfaction because it was rebellion against the "squares" who walked the straight and narrow.

> *When I was about 15, on a Friday night we'd meet up at the Winterburn Pharmacy and either thumb or take a streetcar to the Stanley Theater. Our friend would pay, he was honest (laughs). He'd go upstairs where the exit was on the balcony and open the doors. They had a steel runner with the weights on, like a fire escape. He'd push it down and then we'd all go in, there was a ton of us. Then the usher would come up, he'd see us there. We'd tell the kid, "Hey, if you got any sense you better get outta here." So we'd all sit and watch the show. Then coming out from downtown, you paid the driver in the front of the streetcar when you got off. This one kid we loafed with, he was built—he was a Pitt defensive lineman—and he'd open up the center doors. The bus driver could see us in his mirror, but we'd just jump off, "Hey! See you later." So we went to the show for nothing, bus for nothing. All we had to pay for was a little candy or popcorn.*

The city of Pittsburgh, meanwhile, was experiencing what its politicians called a Renaissance. The Pittsburgh Railways Company sold the Duquesne Gardens to a company that built an apartment house on the site. To replace the Gardens, the city tore down a neighborhood in the lower Hill District to build a civic arena. The folks who lived there, mostly poor African-American families, scrambled to find new homes they could afford.

Greenfield families were also victims of this Renaissance. The city had begun to build the Parkway East some years earlier, and the first leg was already in place, reaching from downtown Pittsburgh's Grant Street to Bates Street in Oakland. Building was halted during the war, but the resultant new prosperity saw The Run torn up by the next leg of the Parkway, which led to the Squirrel Hill Tunnel near Forward Avenue. Building the tunnel was a painstaking process of cutting through solid rock, and work moved along at only eight feet per day. Even though they toiled at such a slow and careful pace, three men were killed by rockslides before the work was done.

The Renaissance also turned empty lots in Greenfield into viable revenue, and attractive brick homes went up along Beechwood Boulevard near the new Parkway, as well as on Bigelow Street in the area realtors called Bigelow Heights.

But the center of life in Greenfield and Hazelwood was still the mill. Residents told time by the sound of the change-of-shift whistles. Businesses and bus routes were determined by how they could best serve the millworker and his family. If a mill siren went off when it wasn't shift time, everyone worried until their loved ones came home safe and sound. Darkness never even fell in Greenfield—the evening skies instead were bathed in the soft pink sulfuric haze of the mill's blast furnace.

There were so many kids. They used to say you had to have ten kids and a dog to live on our street.

Before work on the Squirrel Hill Tunnel was complete, engineers from the State Highway Department realized the tunnel had been made too small for the traffic it would carry.

NEIGHBORHOOD JUMP ROPE JINGLES

Down in the meadow where the green grass grows
There sat Franny as sweet as a rose
She sang, she sang, she sang so sweet
Along came Jerry and kissed her on the cheek
How many kisses did she get?
One, two, three, four...

Cinderella dressed in yella
Went downstairs to meet her fella
On the way her girdle busted
How many people were disgusted?
One, two, three, four...

Lincoln, Lincoln, I been thinkin'
What the heck have you been drinkin'
Smells like whiskey, tastes like wine
Oh my gosh, it's turpentine!

Blue bells, cockle shells,
(Swing the rope back and forth while person jumps over)
Eevy ivy overhead
(Turn the rope overhead)
Go to the kitchen and
Make me a sandwich and
Don't forget the
RED HOT PEPPER!
(Spin the rope as fast as you can)

Greenfield was filled to the brim with baby-boomer kids. Streets were packed with raucous ballgames and strings of kids playing Red Rover. Sidewalks overflowed with girls jumping rope and pushing dolls in tiny baby carriages.

Men on their way home from work shared the sidewalk with little ones playing Mother May I or Red Light Green Light Yellow Light Stop. Magee Field's swimming pool was so full of kids that they often just stood in the water and talked, trying to keep cool, rather than attempting to swim through the crowds. Older boys sat on the city steps under the trees, playing cards and nickel-dime gambling.

We used to build sheds out in the sumac trees up by Fort Black. We could sit on the hill and see J&L, the coke ovens—all of Hazelwood, the rivers and everything.

Pockets of woods held gangs of boys playing Cowboys and Indians, or hiding in homemade shacks where they could fold the Land-O-Lakes butter box into rude pictures or peruse a stash of purloined magazines.

Older boys who lived near the top of Greenfield Avenue loafed at Roosevelt School or in front of the corner stores. Boys from the bottom of The Avenue loafed on the street corners or at St. Rosalia's lyceum, even though the building was now so old it was a fire trap. Girls made their way through gangs of boys to buy a cherry Coke or a comic book at the drugstore.

Our group always stayed at the Winterburn Pharmacy. We never went up the top of the hill, and we never went down the bottom of the hill. They never come down our way and we never went up their way. We got along good.

Often the only time the various gangs got together—other than to fight—was the Fourth of July celebration at Magee Field, where there were three-legged races, egg tosses and bags of candy for every child attending.

A streetcar ride took Greenfield's teenagers to South Park, where they could swim or lie in the sun smeared with baby oil and iodine, working on their tans. Another attraction south of the city, in a suburb of Pittsburgh called Castle Shannon, was a popular dance hall called Linden Grove. The roof of the building was held up by wooden poles carved with hearts and initials of love-struck teens. Everyone from all over the city danced at the Grove, but each neighborhood had its own recognized section of the dance hall. If you were from Greenfield, you hung out in the corner where the Greenfield people were.

School picnics at Kennywood were still the event of the summer, and the excitement began weeks before the kids spotted the big "Laugh in the Dark" lady at the park's entrance. Children with sunburned noses daydreamed about walking around the park carrying prizes they won by knocking over wooden milk bottles. Older boys (and some of their fathers) planned to watch the girls' dresses fly up as they crossed the wooden bridge in front of the Noah's Ark fun house, a wooden boat that rocked from side to side high atop a manmade hill. Mothers packed picnic baskets that fathers would carry to one of the pavilions where they would play cards while the kids ran around—"Watch your sister!"—or sit on the benches and listen to the music.

> *Our big thrill was catching the streetcar to Kennywood Park on school picnic day. The first thing you would see at Kennywood Park would be that big fountain at the pool. My mother would pack a basket, and we'd always sit in the grove by the Jack Rabbit. We'd swim from 12 until 5. Five o'clock we'd come in, starved to death. So we'd eat what she brought—her potato salad, I still remember what she put in it, little chips of bacon, it was delicious. Then we'd ride all night. That was our big vacation.*

As the decade went on, actual vacations became possible for some of Greenfield's working-class families. Lake Erie, closer and more affordable than Atlantic City, was a favorite destination.

> *We used to take the kids up to Presque Isle several times during the summer. They liked the waves. I don't know whether they thought that was the ocean or not. It was good enough for them.*

Other Greenfielders had summer homes in country towns like Butler or Wexford, inherited from parents and grandparents who settled there when they arrived from the old country.

Families could also afford some of the amenities they saw on television, and most Greenfield homes had central heating and refrigerators. There was one other way in which Greenfield mirrored television towns: although a handful of African-American families rented houses or apartments in The Run, there was not one single home in Greenfield owned by a family that was not white. ◆

At this time, there was a tradition among Greenfield girls that, on school picnic day, they would dress alike. This custom was so widespread that two girls in similar outfits would be asked, "Are you going to Kennywood?"

21 | PROSPERITY

Everyone I knew either worked in the mill or worked in a shop that the people from the mill went to. There were a couple of professional people but they were not people that I knew. Definitely a blue-collar town.

Carpenters, electricians, this is where I'm from, you know? My friends worked in the steel mill, worked for the city.

The millworkers union was now the United Steelworkers of America. Greenfield's Jim Thomas, a former sandlot football star, had been district director of the union since before the war. Now the president of the national union was another Greenfield man, Dave McDonald. McDonald's vision was to better the steelworker's condition by increasing his salary and creating shopfloor rules that gave him dignity in the workplace. But to accomplish these goals, a long strike was necessary.

The nationwide strike went on for a 116 days and put many Greenfield families in hardship. Lines formed at the firehouse on Farnsworth Street where coffee-can-sized containers of peanut butter, powdered eggs, oatmeal and powdered milk were distributed to keep families fed. But the burden proved worthwhile when the strike was a resounding success. The men finally made a living wage and could even earn a sabbatical, unheard of in blue-collar professions. Men who worked more than 15 years in the mill were entitled to 13 weeks vacation every five years to recharge the most important tool they used—their bodies.

The success of the steelworkers' strike promised prosperity for all of Greenfield, so it was inevitable that new shops would open on Greenfield Avenue. The Homa family moved from The Run, where they had a greenhouse, to open a flower shop across from St. Rosalia Church. Johnny Sheffo bought Nick Funaro's barbershop. The new prosperity also meant more automobiles, easier to drive on The Avenue since the streetcars had been replaced by buses, and the trolley tracks, laid in cobblestone, were paved over. Still, less than half of Greenfield's residents drove to work. Men on their way to the mill, carrying their trademark shopping bag of workclothes, took the bus or walked.

Prosperity had finally come to Greenfield's immigrant families. Their average income was comfortable and almost everyone was

WHO WAS DAVID J. MCDONALD?

David J. McDonald was born on Flowers Avenue when the area was still called Scotch Bottom, and while his dad was out on strike. He was named after his father, a Welshman who worked at National Tube. His mother, Mary Agnes Kelley, came from a long line of Irish labor leaders.

Talented in sports, music and acting—he majored in drama at Carnegie Tech while working 11-hour shifts at National Tube—Dave was a born leader. The turning point in his life was when he wrangled an introduction to Philip Murray, then vice president of the miners' union. Impressed by Dave's volunteer work with Catholic organizations, Murray hired him on the spot as his private secretary. Under Murray's wing, Dave was groomed for union leadership.

While president of the United Steelworkers of America (CIO), David J. McDonald promoted a "democratic capitalism" which saw management and labor as a partnership between equals, under which laborers provided an honest day's work in exchange for an honest day's pay. McDonald's leadership, both under Philip Murray and as president himself, saw such unheard-of benefits for steelworkers as early diagnostic medical care, overtime pay, monthly pensions at retirement and sabbatical time. As McDonald put it, men who had been eating margarine all their lives were now eating butter.

The corner he loafed on? Lydia Street and Greenfield Avenue, in front of the old McMillin Drug Store.

employed. The poverty rate in Greenfield was half what it was in the rest of the city. Most people owned their homes. Families were still close-knit—there were more married couples in Greenfield than in the average city neighborhood, and the elderly were more likely to live with family than to live alone. Greenfield's residents stayed put—their roots were deep.

In real life, Simon Girty and his wife Catherine had five children, three sons and two daughters: John, Thomas, Prideaux, Nancy Ann and Sarah.

Simon Girty, John Turner's notorious brother, showed up as a television bad guy from time to time, causing trouble for Maverick or harassing TV's Daniel Boone with his villainous fictional sons Hiram, Jeb and Luke. Simon was always defeated because on TV, though the good guys were as violent as the bad guys, the good guys always won. Boys all over the country watched their heros solve their differences with violence, and cap guns and holsters were the preferred Christmas present for most boys and tomboys.

While Pittsburghers acted as guinea pigs for a new invention of Alcoa's—pull-tabs on Iron City beer cans—crime in the city climbed. When national crime rates went up 10%, Pittsburgh's went up 27.3%. Within four years, that rate climbed to an incredible 49.4%. No. 6 Police Station, serving Hazelwood, Greenfield, Squirrel Hill, Shadyside and Point Breeze, blamed the rising crime on narcotics use. Still, arrests for vice infractions were infrequent. In a typical year, No. 6 Station had only 77 arrests for intoxication, by far the lowest in the city.

Alcoholism wasn't any secret. Most of the people on our street were alcoholics. There were four bars within two blocks of each other. I mean, it was a mill town.

Gangs of boys congregated on corners or at Magee Field. Teenagers went to Linden Grove and West View Danceland and listened to their favorite disc jockeys: Chuck Brinkman on KQV, Mad Mike Metro on WZUM, Clark Race on KDKA and Terry Lee on WIXZ. The boys who hung out in front of the corner drugstores a few years ago were now old enough to hang out in the taverns.

Little kids played in the street in front of their houses, and most knew the universal refrain, "Be on the porch when the street lights come on." They seldom played at Magee Field anymore. The ballfield and playground were pretty much taken over by older kids partying on the steps or along the bleachers.

I used to have a big mouth was the thing. I would always have a smart comment. I got the snot beat out of me one time in the locker room at Magee Pool. When I say I got my ass kicked, it wasn't nearly as violent as what you see on the news. A bruised cheek or a black eye, that was it. It wouldn't escalate beyond that.

The Park Theater was closed after the seats had been slashed for the umpteenth time, and the four dances held by St. Rosalia School each year were the only structured community activities available to teens. St. Rosalia's lyceum was torn down and the building's foundation, also taken over by older kids, was now known as The Pit.

Greenfield, never homogenous to begin with, was now so defined that the city of Pittsburgh officially recognized five distinct areas of the neighborhood. Though people might simply say they were from Greenfield, everyone was aware of the part of Greenfield they lived in, and which part they thought was better than the other.

Upper Greenfield. That's what our boss used to always say when we were distributing the Post-Gazette in the morning. He'd say to me, "Hey, you do LOWER Greenfield," and make it sound like, "you scumball."

The Run was still called The Run. Upper and Lower Greenfield were designated as separate areas. The new houses along Bigelow Street were now in Bigelow Heights. Those who lived in the Windsor-Kennebec area usually just said they were from Squirrel Hill.

FIVE DISTINCT SUB-NEIGHBORHOODS
IN GREENFIELD DURING THE 1960s

Area	Population	Number of Houses
Windsor-Kennebec	2660	825
Bigelow Heights	807	216
Central Upper	3674	1050
Run	1084	374
Central Lower	3830	1039

There was a marked difference between saying you were from Greenfield or from Squirrel Hill. To a Pittsburgher, "Squirrel Hill" conjured up ideas of an urbane atmosphere, wealthy people with professional jobs living in beautiful old mansions and sending their 2.5 children to college. Greenfield had a grittier reputation, a family-oriented town of hardworking millhunks who knew their way around a barroom, who went to church on Sunday but never walked away from a street fight.

The business district at the bottom of Murray Avenue in Greenfield was different from the business district on Greenfield Avenue near St. Rosalia Church. Lower Greenfield had a row of family-owned shops, but Upper Greenfield sported chain stores as well: two supermarkets, Giant Eagle and Foodland, and a Baskin-Robbins ice cream store. Lester's Delicatessen sold corned beef sandwiches and six-packs of beer; there was a little variety toy store as well as two drugstores, a veterinarian and a pizza shop.

The veterinarian, I loved him. He was so nice to the animals.

Near Calvary Cemetery there was a laundromat, and a little market at the top of Hazelwood Avenue that sold plants for your garden.

You could do your grocery shopping and the laundry at the same time. I still remember summer nights walking down there, people on their porches, how comfortable that all felt.

Bill Ung's family owned the town's Chinese restaurant, the Tea Garden, famous for its eggrolls. Greenfield boys had their first jobs bagging groceries at the supermarkets or shelling shrimp in the basement of Mr. Ung's restaurant. Of course, the business area was sprinkled with taverns.

The occasional transplant from the suburbs was struck by the differences between Greenfield and suburban neighborhoods. Unlike the suburbs, everyone didn't have a car.

I remember you never heard a car in the middle of the night. If you did, everybody was looking out their window wondering who was out there.

There was a guy lived up on Stanley Street, never owned an automobile. The first day he had the car, first morning he drove the car to work, he came down the street, hit this car and this car and that car, bounced back and forth until finally he went up on the lawn, right over the wall, all the way down the field on the hillside. He just never put any brakes on, I guess he was petrified. I got up to go to work and I'm standing in our kitchen on Haldane Street buttoning my shirt and I look out and I see this car. It went right between two big trees and hit the back fence in our yard and our neighbor's. There was a big garden out beyond the fence, he tore cabbages and everything up. Tore both fences out, and he wound up with the front end of his car sitting in my backyard. And he got out of the car, and he looked around, and he reached in and took his raincoat, put it over his arm, and he walked out. Never came back. He never drove another car, either.

Those who owned a car parked it on the street, not in a driveway. Some of the streets were so narrow that two-way traffic required one car to pull over to let the other pass. Unlike the suburbs, washers and especially dryers were luxuries, not necessities. Plenty of folks used the laundromat or hung their clothes in backyards stretched end to end with clotheslines.

As Greenfield's reputation slowly climbed, Hazelwood's reputation got worse. Hazelwood had always been racially mixed and that had never been a problem. Folks had known each other's families for generations and neighbors got along well. But when the lower Hill District was torn down to make way for the Civic Arena and folks who lived in that area scrambled to find a new place to live, many moved to Hazelwood because it was racially diverse and inexpensive. Over that decade, the town's white population decreased nearly 20% while its African-American population increased 20%.

When civil rights activist Dr. Martin Luther King Jr. was shot, riots broke out in black neighborhoods of major cities all over the country, and Pittsburgh was no exception. Hazelwood might have escaped this strife except for two factors—one, many of the people in Hazelwood were now strangers to each other, and two, newspapers reported that boys from Greenfield were driving through Hazelwood hollering racial epithets through their car windows, raising the tension to a fever pitch.

As far back as anyone could remember, there had always been a rivalry between Greenfield and Hazelwood. It had to do with economics, as did the rivalry between Greenfield and Squirrel Hill. A boy from Hazelwood who dated a girl from Greenfield might be razzed by his neighbors about his "rich girlfriend from Greenfield." A family from Greenfield didn't move to Hazelwood, and if they did, their neighbors cautioned them about moving to a place "beneath them." Families moving up in the world bought homes in Squirrel Hill or, lacking the funds for that, in West Mifflin, an affordable suburb south of the city.

But most Greenfield folks stayed where they were. Many lived in the same homes their grandparents bought when they first moved to America. Someone who lived in the area for a long time might say "I'm not from Greenfield, I've only lived here 30 years," and no one would disagree. Roots were deep. As children grew and got married, they moved in with family or bought houses on neighboring streets. Grandfathers stopped by to see the grandchildren on the way home from work. Daughters-in-law helped with the family's gardening. Sunday suppers were prepared by the matriarch for everyone in the family, and everyone was expected to attend.

Protest rallies against the Vietnam War were held in Market Square, while long-haired boys in love beads and girls with flowing dresses danced to their own drummers on Schenley Park's Flagstaff Hill. During the same year, No. 6 Police Station recorded the second highest rate of burglary and the third highest rate of auto theft in the city.

The pizza place at the corner of Greenfield Avenue was always getting robbed. It changed hands a couple of times but it got robbed no matter who owned it.

A full 20% of the arrests in Pittsburgh were juveniles. The "love and peace" hippie era seemed to leave only one mark on Greenfield—drugs.

It was easy for kids to buy cigarettes. All they needed was the 35 cents. They could pick them up at the corner store as long as they bought their mother's brand and said they were for her, or they could use a cigarette machine like the one at the fire house on Winterburn Street.

The rumor would float around, "We're getting a pack of cigarettes," and three or four of us would meet somewhere and smoke all 20 of them at once. It wasn't like we did it for pleasure, we did it because we weren't supposed to.

Liquor was a little tougher to get, but there was usually an older kid around who could get served or knew someone who could. And now there were all these new pills to try and weeds to smoke.

An older boy stole wine out of the church. I was a little kid, they usually didn't want me hanging around, but for some reason they invited me this time. "We got wine, come on, we're gonna drink it and smoke cigarettes." My mother knew I was into something and came looking for me, so I didn't get any wine. And I got whipped. But I do remember having a cigarette for the first time.

Older kids sat on the city steps with the younger kids who followed them around, begging to be corrupted. They taught them how to smoke cigarettes while scaring them with wild ghost stories about the neighborhood, showing them abandoned houses "where a man hacked his wife to death with an ax" or telling them how "Old King Kearcher was a hunchback, and when he died his hump wouldn't fit in the casket, so they buried it in Green Grass and when it's dark—see, do you see it floating up there?"

Parents, even those who weren't Catholic, sent children who were discipline problems to Catholic school to get "straightened out" now that public schools were becoming so liberal—and integrated. At Taylor Allderdice High School, discipline had become a joke, and the principal of one of the worst schools in the city was brought in to restore order. He walked through the cafeteria and hallways, he knew the majority of the students by name, and he was known to chase kids all the way to Frick Park if he caught them cutting class. But it looked like getting the upper hand with the students at Allderdice might be a taller order than he bargained for. ◆

MISBEHAVING | 22

In a Catholic school, if you didn't want to go to school, you had to miss the whole day. Anybody missing just one class was asking to be caught because the schools were too small.

For the Catholic girls who attended St. Paul's Cathedral High School in Oakland or Sacred Heart High School in Shadyside— now that St. Rosalia High School had closed down—and for the Catholic boys who attended Central Catholic High School in Oakland, high school was an extension of grade school as far as discipline was concerned. Cutting school was nearly impossible because the minute someone noticed you were missing, the principal would call your house looking for you. Central Catholic was also run in the same manner it had been a generation before, and this commitment extended to hiring a former military man as Prefect of Discipline.

Some Catholic kids were able to convince their parents that they would not be corrupted at a public school. Their argument was reinforced by the fact that the mills were cutting back and money was getting tight while, at the same time, tuition in parochial schools was rising rapidly. Many of these students joined the kids from public grade schools on the first day of freshman year at Taylor Allderdice High School.

For most students, the first day at Allderdice was an awakening. They came from smaller schools to a huge school with 2,000 students, where their teachers weren't likely to notice if they misbehaved, and were even less likely to call their parents.

It was the numbers that freaked me out at first. Going from a place where you literally know everybody in the school to someplace ten times that size.

Though the mills weren't hiring, many of the students from Greenfield and some of the other mill towns didn't plan to go to college and didn't care about getting an education. They were teenagers, and they were in school to have fun.

Cutting school at Allderdice was easy and, for the most part, tolerated. During a school day, students could always be found sitting on the grassy hill outside the school on Shady Avenue, walking to Frick Park, hanging out on Murray Avenue or eating

A few Greenfield students also attended Bishop Boyle High School, a coeducational school in nearby Homestead.

bacon and eggs at Nick's, the latest of a series of little diners on Forward Avenue that replaced the Hot Puppie as a teen hangout.

The first day at Allderdice, the principal said to us, "If you want an education, this is one of the best schools in southwestern Pennsylvania. But if you don't, there's just too many of you. So, do what you want." And I heard, "Do what you want." So I did, I missed as many classes as I could.

Hall passes. I had tablets of them. I got them from a senior who worked in the counselor's office. (Laughs.) I signed my counselor's name better than he did.

I used to cut third period and go have bacon and eggs every morning. It was electric shop one year and I cut 62 days in a row. They finally caught up with me but they just said, "Go back to class." I went back but nothing happened, so I started cutting second period.

Most of the freshmen at Allderdice had spent first grade through eighth grade with the same kids in every class. Now, because of the size and diversity of the high school, these students were surrounded with kids they had never seen before. Many were meeting people of different racial and economic backgrounds for the first time in their lives. Some students adjusted and even thrived in this atmosphere.

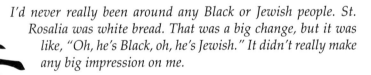

I'd never really been around any Black or Jewish people. St. Rosalia was white bread. That was a big change, but it was like, "Oh, he's Black, oh, he's Jewish." It didn't really make any big impression on me.

For others, it seemed natural and safe to band tightly together with kids from their own neighborhood. Teenagers from rival Greenfield gangs became friends out of necessity, to fight what they perceived as a common foe.

Greenfield was a tough neighborhood, you didn't mess with anybody in Greenfield. We all stuck together.

For some years now, there had been a phenomenon in the gang rivalry. It was Friday's tomb. Each Friday the 13th, a one-night truce was called at Friday's tomb in Calvary Cemetery. Teenagers from Greenfield, Hazelwood and other rival areas would party together, telling stories to the younger kids about Friday's ghost, which was sure to come out at midnight.

This same mentality—the party truce—existed at Allderdice. Nearly every winter day, Greenfield kids would stand on the hill above the bus stop where the Lincoln Place kids waited to go home, firing snowballs and urging them to fight. But there was an area on Allderdice's grounds near the smokestack to the boiler that the students referred to as "The Stacks." The Stacks were recognized by students as the domain of teens from Greenfield and Lincoln Place, a neutral territory where they could get together and "get high."

The fights and altercations that occurred between the people from Greenfield and Lincoln Place were much more violent than any of the other combinations. (Laughs.) They would sit around and get high together, though.

Someone from Greenfield would get in a fight with somebody from Homewood and it would escalate. There would be people saying, "We're gonna kick those niggers' asses," and then in shop class I'd hear Black people saying, "We're gonna whomp some honky ass after school." In situations like that, the people from Lincoln Place and Greenfield would exhibit solidarity.

Kids from Squirrel Hill often didn't associate with kids from Greenfield and Lincoln Place, and would usually avoid The Stacks, considering it a hangout for toughs. This is not to say that there weren't drug users from Squirrel Hill, only that their activities were different. They had bigger homes and, often, both parents had professional jobs, leaving the house free for cutting school and partying. But they would be more likely to play hacky sack than get into fights.

There were just as many drugs in Squirrel Hill as there were in Greenfield. And there was a certain amount of money. When we went to a party in Greenfield, we ended up trashing the place. You didn't want anybody at your house. But in Squirrel Hill, it was like, "You destroyed this room, that's okay, we can fix it up again."

S̶moking marijuana for many of the students was a daily occurrence, and there was little effort made to hide this practice. Cigarette papers and pocket bongs were available at Heads Together, a "head shop" left over from Squirrel Hill's hippie days and located just blocks from the school. Often, teens chose drugs over alcohol simply because they were easier to obtain.

At Allderdice, the extracurricular activities consisted of smoking a couple joints at lunchtime and going back to class (laughs), with a much better attitude.

When I went to Allderdice, you could still get Quaaludes and stuff like that. Cocaine wasn't very prevalent, at least among the circles I traveled. Mostly it was just smoking grass. If you looked for it, you could find LSD or mushrooms or whatever.

A head shop is a place where drug paraphernalia is sold. In those days, Heads Together sold cigarette papers, pipes and bongs (pipes with a water filter) to smoke marijuana and hashish, as well as Rush (little bottles of butyl nitrite) and Whippets (small metal containers of nitrous oxide).

House parties were less and less common in Greenfield, but there were other shared endeavors among the public and parochial school students. Fort Black had been converted to a playground called Hammer Field. Underage kids were still drinking there, as they had decades before. But instead of marshmallow roasts with a bottle of Virginia Dare wine, there were "keggers."

A kegger was a floating beer party organized by underage kids. A kid who looked old enough to buy alcohol would get a keg of beer and take it to a predetermined location, often a hidden area in a park or playground. News of the party was spread by word of mouth. Attendees would pay an entrance fee of a few dollars, for which they received a plastic cup for their beer. Cups were marked or held tightly, because if you needed another one you had to pay another entrance fee.

I didn't hang out at Hammer Field, although I went to keggers there. There was a street in that area where you walk through the woods, down a hill, and suddenly you're on old cracked asphalt where they literally closed the street off. People would have keg parties down there. Being inebriated, I can't remember exactly where it was.

I was 16 the first time I went to a kegger. It was sponsored by people from Greenfield, but it was in Frick Park. We cut school, walked straight through the park on Beechwood, then down a hill into the section of Frick Park in Swissvale. The kegger was in a hidden grove down there, because it was a clandestine thing.

Pennsylvania drivers licenses at this time were simply text printed on plain yellow paper. Anyone with a pen and a steady hand could alter their birth year to make themselves old enough to buy beer.

Teenagers from public and parochial schools who were bent on illegal activity shared another common ground—Magee Field. Older kids hung out there, and alcohol and drugs were easily accessible. Evenings were spent drinking a case of beer or two on the playground steps and then fighting, playing inebriated games of softball or basketball, or breaking into the pool to swim.

I didn't feel like I fit in. So I used to go to Magee and get high or get drunk, and then you fit in.

You could walk down to Mike's Bar or the Win Green for beer—two six-packs was $4 or $5—take it up Magee and drink it. I started getting served when I was 16 years old.

Street drugs like heroin or cocaine were not as available in Greenfield as they were in the East Liberty or Larimer Avenue sections of the city. At Magee Field, prescription drugs were common and easy to obtain, and those who abused these "FDA-approved" drugs considered heroin and cocaine users to be "drug addicts."

Greenfield, along with certain other neighborhoods like Brookline, boasted a reputation as a place to buy illegal prescription drugs.

If you'd mention Greenfield, you got a certain amount of respect, because there was this drug culture thing going on. You used that as a way to get into other people's cliques. "He's okay, he's from Greenfield."

It was common knowledge among drug users which doctors were willing to write prescriptions in exchange for a sob story and the price of an office visit. Older drug users got prescriptions for Percodan or Quaaludes, which they would use themselves or trade on the streets. Dilaudid, one of these prescription drugs, was so popular it could be used almost as currency.

I met my husband at a party celebrating his parole. He was busted for drugs. I never remember him actually doing drugs, but I remember every time I would say to him, "I wish we had more money," he would say, "I know how I could get some, fast," and I knew that meant he would go out dealing again.

The Corner Pocket, a pool hall right across the bridge on Murray Avenue to Squirrel Hill, was frequented by young people from all over the city. Unlike Mike's Bar in Greenfield, new faces were seen at the Corner Pocket every day. The two older Italian men who ran the pool hall tried to keep it a family place and had rules against drinking and swearing. The regulars, who spent as much time loafing outside the pool hall as they did inside it, respected the owners enough not to use or sell drugs in front of them. But there was nothing the owners could do about people using or dealing drugs outside their establishment, and regulars joked that there were more drugs available at the Corner Pocket than at the Murray Pharmacy.

I was drawn to dark things, and the pool hall was one of them. There were seedy people; there was something going on there that wasn't right, had to happen in this dark place. It was so interesting.

Police occasionally swept the sidewalk and arrested people hanging out in front of the Corner Pocket, but they were taken to the police station and given a slap on the wrist. The same punishment was given for underage drinking at Magee Field.

We used to get chased down Magee, we'd have barrels down Magee and the police would come. They'd take you to the station and charge you with underage drinking, which was $35, or obstructing pedestrian traffic, which was another $35. It was citations. So it became a joke. After a few times, I didn't even run anymore.

Officers who encountered a group of teenagers drinking in Frick Park would often say, "We don't want to write out all these citations. Why don't you just go on home," and simply confiscate the beer and disperse the crowd.

While Dick Caliguiri was mayor, vandals hit Magee Field late one night—again—this time causing $77,000 worth of damage to the pool and bathhouse. The mayor announced plans to rebuild. Magee Field gained a beautiful complex along Greenfield Avenue that held a gym and a senior center, which the mayor's mother attended with pride.

The Greenfield Organization was created, a civic group that brought a health center to town to replace the local doctors who had retired. They also convinced Port Authority of Allegheny County to create a direct bus route to Carnegie Mellon University and the University of Pittsburgh, giving unemployed steelworkers and their children easier access to a college education.

For a while, Greenfield even boasted its very own organized street gang, the Irish Lynch Mob, complete with baggy clothes, team clothing—Boston Celtics or Notre Dame—and trademark green bandannas, their girlfriends sporting "big hair" and swigging Colter-yahn iced tea. On Sunday mornings, they would sometimes attend Mass together at St. Rosalia, sitting in the last pew by the door and joining the congregation for communion. Though city police had thorough records on the gang, few people in the neighborhood were afraid of them. Children called them "Homey-Gs." ♦

The Town Today |

There's a provincialism about Greenfield. People seem to maintain a closeness to the neighborhood no matter where they move to. And people don't move in and out of Greenfield the way they do out of Moon Township or Mount Lebanon or any of these other places around Allegheny County. People tend to move into Greenfield and then sink down roots and stay there.

So how do we leave Greenfield at the end of the 20th century?

At night, the skies are dark instead of pink because the steel mills are gone. What happened to the mills? Your answer will depend on whom you ask. The steel companies insist that they were eager to keep the mills running and simply lacked the capital to meet environmental regulations and union wages. Community activists reply that the steel companies had no intention of keeping the millhunks at work and diverted their capital to real estate, chemicals, oil—any business or industry that required less investment for higher profit. This second theory does seem to be supported by the fact that U.S. Steel changed its name to USX at the same time it put more than 100,000 steelworkers in the tri-state area out of work.

Now that the economic situation is changed, I see some homogenization in the neighborhood, where you have professional people filtering in. Blue-collar jobs are not out there, not to the extent that they once were.

The largest Pittsburgh employers are now the University of Pittsburgh, with all its hospitals and other facilities, and the local, state and federal government. Two of the top ten employers in the city are service industries: Giant Eagle grocery stores and Kaufmann's department stores. If you live in Greenfield, you are as likely now to live next door to a musician or a banker as you are a retired steelworker.

My dad's a mechanic. My mom's an underwriter.

My dad's a human resource director and my mom's a nurse practitioner.

High school kids might work summer jobs at Kennywood or at a mall, but even the children of laborers usually plan to continue their education in college or trade school.

Magee Field remains a place where kids hang out to get drunk or high. There were times in the past the pool was forced to close while maintenance crews picked up broken wine bottles and empty beer cans strewn about the park. The young people who loaf at Magee Field still have little concern about consequences and are known to tilt their beers to friends driving by.

I feel perfectly safe in Greenfield during the day. At night, I would not walk down by Magee if you paid me.

Neighborhood vandals are sometimes cocky enough to spray-paint their own names alongside scrawled obscenities. Residents are especially wary on the night before Halloween, commonly known as Devil's Night.

The corner stores selling deli meats and penny candy that dotted Greenfield's side streets have all been converted to houses or apartments. Mary Burns' Greenfield Grill has undergone a few transformations, but it is still a tavern, and you will still see men standing on the corner outside it. And many of the same boys who sipped cherry Cokes at the soda fountain of Chuck Prokopovitsh's Winterburn Pharmacy now chug beer in the very same spot.

The nuclei of most gangs can be traced back to early boyhood, when living close together provided the first opportunities for social contacts... The gangs grew up on the corner and remained there with remarkable persistence from early boyhood until the members reached their late 20s or early 30s... Frequently movement out of the district does not take the corner boy away from his corner. On any evening on almost any corner one finds corner boys who have come in from other parts of the city or from suburbs to be with their old friends. The residence of the corner boy may also change within the district, but nearly always he retains his allegiance to his original corner.
—William Foote Whyte, "Street Corner Society"

This is the case with many of the bars on The Avenue. Most have their regulars who stop after work to talk, play darts or pinball, and "get a nice buzz." That group might leave around eight or nine o'clock when a second, more rowdy group of regulars arrives. Fights aren't an everyday occurrence, but they certainly aren't uncommon. It's a rare evening that a stranger enters one of Greenfield's local

SOME ASPECTS OF WHAT SOCIOLOGISTS CALL "CORNER CULTURE"

- When a boy from the corner is looking for one of his friends, he goes to the corner rather than to his friend's home.

- Boys and even men are often known by nicknames, and men can drink with each other for years without knowing the other's given name or last name.

- Many men stay on the corner even after they are married.

- After work, a man will often stop at the tavern nearest the corner he loafed on as a youth. He will sit at the same table or same corner of the bar, and everyone knows who sits where. They know not to sit in each other's places.

- A stranger is not welcomed unless they are known to someone in the group.

- A favor done contains an implicit expected favor from the other, and this is understood by both parties.

bars. If they do, it's as obvious to them as to everyone else that they "don't belong."

New immigrants from Russia and from Asian countries are beginning to move into homes in Upper Greenfield, and the neighborhood is a little more homogenous than it was before. Still, outsiders who marry into Greenfield families, especially former suburbanites, sometimes also feel at first that they "don't belong." It can be an adjustment to observe the tradition and ritual still maintained in many Greenfield homes.

> When my husband and I got our first car, his whole family had to go with us to buy the car. And he became the designated driver when his dad needed something. They had never owned a car.

Extended families live near each other and drop in at each other's houses daily to visit with mom and dad, sit on the porch, maybe have a few beers. No one calls first—it's unheard of and unnecessary. Every family member is expected to attend holiday gatherings and, often, Sunday dinners. If a family member is remodeling, moving or doing anything that requires labor, other members of the family are expected to help, the older women preparing meals while the men and younger women paint or hang drywall. Going out to dinner doesn't mean Poli's Restaurant, but instead one of Greenfield's Chinese restaurants or pizza shops, or maybe a trip down Brown's Hill to the Waterfront Mall.

St. Rosalia Church was combined by the Diocese of Pittsburgh with two other Catholic churches, St. Joachim in The Run and the former St. Philomena in Squirrel Hill. The priests at St. Rosalia are very different from what they used to be. Parishioners wonder whether the pastor dyes his blond hair, and remark that they never had a priest before who wore an earring. They remember with horror the morning one of the priests used a Terrible Towel to wipe his hands during Mass on Superbowl Sunday.

Greenfield School's facilities, which include two gyms, an auditorium and a swimming pool, are now shared with students from Oakland and Homewood. Catholic children continue to attend parochial schools, spending kindergarten through eighth grade at St. Rosalia School. The girls wear uniforms, little white polo shirts with plaid skirts and white bobby socks, and the boys wear dress pants with a shirt and tie—a dress code the students are told is necessary to encourage good behavior.

> At lunch, all the girls sat at one table and all the boys sat at another table. None of the girls ever wanted to sit at the end of the table, that was like the kiss of death because you couldn't hear all the conversations. We would have certain days of the week that people would sit on the end. The boys would talk about a car they liked, about golfing and stuff. But they weren't actually talking about golfing. It was disgusting.

Most of these children will continue to wear uniforms as they attend the alma mater of their parents, the boys at Central Catholic High School and girls at Oakland Catholic.

St. Rosalia School is still entirely white, and most of its students are at least part Irish, Italian or German. Though generations of intermarriage have made knowing your ethnic background more of a challenge, most grade school students know which "old country" their ancestors were from.

> I'm Polish, German, Hungarian and Pennsylvania Dutch on my dad's side, and what else? Irish, I think. Yeah, I'm a little bit Irish on my dad's side.

> I'm Croation, Slovak, Hungarian, Polish, Carpatho-Russian and Mongolian.

> I think my son is the only kid in his class that isn't related to somebody else.

Ethnic traditions are still observed in Greenfield, especially at holidays. Irish families get together to make the rounds of the neighborhood bars to celebrate St. Patrick's Day. Slovak families share oplatky at Vilija, their Christmas Eve supper.

> We pick up my grandma on Christmas Eve and have a traditional dinner, no meat but pierogies and haluski and stuff like that. And then we have a tradition that you can't eat until the first star appears.

My mom puts hay on the table and it gets in all the food. I don't know why she does that.

School picnics are well attended, as are Kennywood's nationality days, when Italians or Slovaks from all over the city meet at the park to celebrate their unique heritage.

Billy Conn had one last fight that made the papers. He and Mary Louise were in a convenience store near their home early one morning when Billy overheard a young man threaten the clerk at the register with a gun. Billy, 72 years old at the time, wrestled the would-be robber to the floor and probably would have held him if a newspaper rack hadn't crashed down on them. When police arrived, however, Billy handed them a couple of clues—the culprit's sweatshirt and one of his shoes.

Surprisingly, through all its changes, Greenfield's reputation as a rough-and-ready town has remained much the same as it was in the days when John Turner's cork-and-gun club stirred up the neighborhood.

But it *is* a little tougher to stand in your doorway, take a long, hard hit off that jug and shoot a mess of squirrels for supper. ♦

The street in Oakland that used to run by the Duquesne Gardens is now called Billy Conn Boulevard.

AFTERWORD

Do you remember the old story of the five blind men and the elephant? An elephant came to town and five blind men surrounded it, each trying to describe what an elephant is like. The man nearest the trunk said an elephant is like a tree branch. A man near the tail described an elephant as a rope. One man, near a leg, said an elephant is like a tree trunk. A man at the elephant's side said an elephant resembles a wall. The blind man near the ear told the group that an elephant is like a huge fan.

Sometimes history can be like that. I have written this story as I see it. Other writers may have other viewpoints. I encourage you to read them all, and draw your own conclusions. ♦

Anita Kulina
July 2003

A Partial List of Sources

Allegheny County's Americans by Choice, Ed. Margaret E. Hartford, American Service Institute of Allegheny County, 1944

"Area lawmaker had role in Johnson case," Roger Stuart, *Pittsburgh Post-Gazette.* January 12, 1999

"Ball field in New Homestead defiled by vandals' graffiti," Johnna A. Pro, *Pittsburgh Post-Gazette,* October 12, 1999

The Bicentennial History of Pittsburgh and Allegheny County, George Swetnam, Historical Record Association, 1955

"Billy Conn," *Pittsburgh Magazine,* December 1985

"Billy Conn lends a fist against thief," *Pittsburgh Post-Gazette,* January 11, 1990

"The Boxer and the Blonde," Frank DeFord, *Sports Illustrated,* June 17, 1985

"Caliguiri's Legacy," *Pittsburgh Post-Gazette,* May 6, 1998

Captive in the Wild, Robert V. McCarthy, Pub. Robert V. McCarthy, 1997

"The Capture of Fort Duquesne," *http://www.digitalhistory.org* [accessed July 28, 1999]

"A conversation with Michael Murphy," Ruth Hammond, *Pittsburgh City Paper,* July 1, 1998

Correspondence of Samuel D. Rich, 1920s, State Police Records, Pennsylvania State Archives, Harrisburg, PA

Crossroads, Descriptions of Western Pennsylvania 1720-1829, Ed. John W. Harpster, University of Pittsburgh Press, 1986

"CRP Neighborhood Profile, Greenfield," *Community Renewal Program,* Department of City Planning, Pittsburgh PA, 1963

A Cycle of Outrage, America's Reaction to the Juvenile Delinquent in the 1950s, James Gilbert, Oxford University Press, 1986

The Damnation of Simon Girty, Harold Frederic, Pub. Harold Frederic, 1991

Delinquent Boys: The Culture of the Gang, Albert K. Cohen, The Free Press, 1955

"A disturbing letter came my way," Lynn M. Anderson, *Greenfield Grapevine,* September 1987

"Drought ended Monongahela Indian culture," *Pittsburgh Post-Gazette,* November 11, 2002

"Duquesne Gardens: City's premier exhibition hall," Henry Peter Gribbin, *Pittsburgh Golden Times,* October 1996

The Early Historical Development of Hazelwood, Joan Miller, History Department, University of Pittsburgh, 1966

"Earliest Settlements in the Fifteenth Ward of Pittsburgh," Mrs. S. Kussart, *Western Pennsylvania Historical Magazine,* Vol. 7, 1924

Early Land Marks and Names of Old Pittsburgh, Annie Clark Miller, Pittsburgh Chapter, Daughters of the American Revolution, 1924

Ethnic America, Thomas Sowell, Basic Books, Inc., 1981

Ethnic Families in America: Patterns and Variations, Ed. Charles H. Mindel and Robert W. Habenstein, Elsevier, 1988

Fag an Bealach: The Irish Contribution to America and in particular to Western Pennsylvania, Margaret E. Maloney, United Irish Societies Bicentennial Committee of Western Pennsylvania, 1977

The Fifties, David Halberstam, Villard Books, 1993

The Fifties: The Way We Really Were, Douglas T. Miller and Marion Nowak, Doubleday and Company, Inc., 1977

"Fort Black, Greenfield's Civil War Connection," Thomas A. Baker, *Greenfield Grapevine*, February 1988

The Gang, Frederic M. Thrasher, The University of Chicago Press, 1927

The Good Old Days, They Were Terrible, Otto L. Bettmann, Random House, 1974

"The Great Depression," *www.pbs.org* [accessed June 17, 1999]

Greenfield Crime Statistics, City of Pittsburgh Bureau of Police, Crime Analysis Unit, 1988-1990

"Greenfield History," *Greenfield Grapevine*, December 1996, January 1997

"Greenfield Memories," JoAnne Klimovich Harrop, *Greenfield Grapevine*, March 1996, April 1996, May 1996, June 1996, September 1996, October 1996

Greenfield Organization Newsletter, 1968

"Greenfield Presbyterian Church Celebrates 100th Birthday," JoAnne Klimovich Harrop, *Greenfield Grapevine*, April 1997

"Greenfield residents remember when," Sharon Gruss, *Greenfield Grapevine*, November 1993

Greenfield School Rededication, William O. Brim, unpublished document, 1989

A Guidebook to Historic Western Pennsylvania, George Swetnam and Helene Smith, University of Pittsburgh Press, 1976

The Hazelwood Community, Anonymous, Gladstone School, unpublished document, not dated, circa 1967

Historic Highways of America, Volume 2: Indian Thoroughfares, Archer Butler Hulbert, AMS Press, 1972

The History of Greenfield, Anonymous, Historical Society of Western Pennsylvania, unpublished document, date unknown

History of Pittsburgh and Environs, George Thornton Fleming, American Historical Society, 1922

History of the old 23rd Ward, Pittsburgh, PA, Mrs. A.D. Price, unpublished document, date unknown

History of the Girtys, Consul Willshire Butterfield, Robert Clarke & Co., 1890

"History of the Squirrel Hill Christian Church," *Greenfield Grapevine*, December 1995

"Homa Floral Shop Creates Beautiful Arrangements," *Greenfield Grapevine*, January 1998

"Homer's service station has come a long way since 1951," JoAnne Klimovich Harrop, *Greenfield Grapevine*, November 1995

Homestead, William Serrin, Vintage Books, 1993

Hoods, the Story of the Ku Klux Klan, Robert P. Ingalls, G.P. Putnam's Sons, 1979

"How goes the renaissance?," *Pittsburgh Post-Gazette*, October 16, 1971

How the Irish Became White, Noel Ignatiev, Routledge, NY, 1995

Imagine Pittsburgh When..., Joseph B.C. White, Conservation Consultants, 1980

The Immigrant Church and Community, Pittsburgh's Slovak Catholics and Lutherans, 1880-1915, June Granatir Alexander, University of Pittsburgh Press, 1987

In Memory of the Early Settlers of Squirrel Hill and Their Descendants, Samuel Worth Stewart, Samuel S. Brown and W. Harry Brown, Mary S. Brown Memorial M.E. Church, Pittsburgh Printing Company, 1905

"Indian interpreter, liaison reviled as savage in a civilized land," Mike Sajna, *Pittsburgh Tribune-Review,* March 1, 1992

Indian Paths of Pennsylvania, Paul A.W. Wallace, Pennsylvania Historical and Museum Commission, 1965

Indians in Pennsylvania, Paul A.W. Wallace, Pennsylvania Historical and Museum Commission, 1964

"Industrial Control Reports #256," *James True Associates, Washington, DC, March 11, 1939,* State Police Records, Pennsylvania State Archives, Harrisburg, PA

Introduction to Juvenile Delinquency: Youth and the Law, James T. Carey and Patrick D. McAnany, Prentice-Hall, 1984

"Kennywood History," *www.kennywood.com* [accessed November 24, 1999]

"King of All the Marvels," Grantland Rice, *Collier's,* February 20, 1926

Ku Klux Klan literature and voting results, 1920s-1930s, State Police Records, Pennsylvania State Archives, Harrisburg, PA

The Land in the Fork, Pittsburgh 1753-1914, Laura C. Frey, Dorrance & Company, 1955

Legends, Lies and Cherished Myths of American History, Richard Shenkman, William Morrow & Company, Inc., 1988

"Lenni-Lenape Indians were earliest area residents," Angela Dyer, *Pittsburgh Post-Gazette,* June 30, 1998

Life and Architecture in Pittsburgh, James D. Van Trump, Pittsburgh History and Landmarks Foundation, 1983

List of Greenfield memories, Virginia Walsh, unpublished document, 1996

Man of Steel, George Kelly and Edwin Beachler, North American Book Company, 1954

Migration Routes and Settlement Patterns 1607-1890, George K. Schweitzer, unpublished document

"'A Monster So Brutal:' Simon Girty and the Degenerative Myth of the American Frontier," Daniel P. Barr, from *Essays in History,* Corcoran Department of History at the University of Virginia, 1998

Old Homes of New Americans, The Country and the People of the Austro-Hungarian Monarchy and Their Contribution to the New World, Francis E. Clark, Riverside Press, 1913, *www.iarelative.com/oldhomes/index.html* [accessed February 3, 2000]

"Old Mansion in Hazelwood Retains Many Memories," unknown, undated Pittsburgh newspaper, circa 1909

"Pittsburgh," Ed. Roy Lubove, *New Viewpoints,* 1976

Pittsburgh, A Chronological and Documentary History 1682-1976, Robert I. Vexler, Oceana Publications, 1977

Pittsburgh, A Sketch of Its Early Social Life, Charles W. Dahlinger, G.P. Putnam's Sons, 1916

Pittsburgh: The Story of an American City, Stefan Lorant, Doubleday, 1964

Pittsburgh and the Pittsburgh Spirit, Chamber of Commerce of Pittsburgh, 1928

Pittsburgh in 1816, Carnegie Library of Pittsburgh, 1926

Pittsburgh in the Year Eighteen Hundred and Twenty-Six, S. Jones, Johnston & Stockton, 1826

Pittsburgh, Our City, Nancy Ward Balderose, School District of Pittsburgh, 1991

Pittsburgh Then and Now, Arthur G. Smith, University of Pittsburgh Press, 1990

"Pittsburgh's forgotten merry-go-rounds," Paul S. Korol, *Pittsburgh Senior News,* April 1999

Pittsylvania Country, George Swetnam, Duell, Sloan and Pearce, 1951

"The Point: 'Diondega,'" George P. Donehoo, *www.clpgh.org/exhibit/neighborhoods/point/point_n491.html* [accessed August 31, 1999]

"Revisiting the Mound-Builder Controversy," Thomas Garlinghouse, *History Today,* September 2001

Right Here in Squirrel Hill, Hodge McIlvain Eagleson, Jackson Church Press, 1953

St. Joachim records, Diocese of Pittsburgh, Diocesan Historical Archives, unpublished document, 1951

"Saline Street area is rich in history," Rich Kleppick, *Greenfield Grapevine,* date unknown

"Schenley Park Donated by Girl Whose Romance Shocked a Queen," Bernice Shine, *Pittsburgh Sun-Telegraph,* September 14, 1941

Scrapbook of School Histories, Pittsburgh Public Schools Archival Survey Project, December 2, 1982

Senator John Heinz Regional History Center, Pittsburgh, Pennsylvania, various exhibits, 1996-1999

The Shadow of the Mills, S.J. Kleinberg, University of Pittsburgh Press, 1989

A Short History of Pittsburgh 1758-1908, Samuel Harden Church, DeVinne Press, 1908

Street Corner Society, William Foote Whyte, University of Chicago Press, 1955

"Squirrel Hill," Margaret A. Frew, *Western Pennsylvania Historical Magazine,* Vol. 12, pp. 242-256, 1929

"The Squirrel Hill Brick Company and the Incredible Mr. Edwin Collins," Thomas A. Baker, *Greenfield Grapevine,* April 1988

"The Squirrel Hill Story," Leon Miller, *Carnegie Magazine,* February 1971

The Squirrel Hill Story, Vignettes of How It All Began, Sarah B. Mishelevich, unpublished manuscript, 1994

The Steel Workers, John A. Fitch, University of Pittsburgh Press, 1989

The Story of Pittsburgh, Rosemary K. Coffey, School District of Pittsburgh, Pennsylvania, 1986

Stringtown on the Pike, John Fulton Stuart Collins Jr., East Liberty Chamber of Commerce, 1966

"Tales Along the Trails," Jerry Kerchner, *Common Ground Magazine,* Summer 2001

A Topographical Description of the Western Territory of North America, Third Edition, Gilbert Imlay, London, J. Debrett, 1797

"The Trolleys of Yesteryear," Thomas A. Baker, *Greenfield Grapevine,* date unknown

Undaunted Courage, Stephen E. Ambrose, Simon & Schuster, 1996

"Vignettes," Robert B. VanAtta, *Pittsburgh Tribune-Review,* April 5; May 10, 17; June 21, 28; July 5, 12, 19, 26; August 3, 9, 23; September 13, 20, 27; November 15, 30; December 10, 13, 1998; June 20, 1999

"Warrior prepares for battle," Jackie Fair, *Pittsburgh Tribune-Review,* July 31, 1997

"Welcome, Englishmen," Paul Kennedy, *Pittsburgh Tribune-Review,* May 9, 1999

Where Else But Pittsburgh?, George Swetnam, Davis and Wade, 1958

"The whistle," by Gloria Crum, *Greenfield Grapevine,* May 1989

"White gang worries police," John Temple, *Pittsburgh Tribune-Review,* July 4, 1993

"You Had to Ask," by Chris Potter, *Pittsburgh City Paper,* December 3, 1998; March 31, 1999; April 8, 1998; June 17, 1998; July 1, 1998; September 10, 1998; February 18, 1999; June 3, 10, 24, 1999; May 4, 2000

Thanks!

Heartfelt thanks to the following people who shared their stories with us.

Brian Bakey
Melissa Bakey
Al Casciato
Helen Creen
Mary Florkowski
Ken Girty
Anne Gruber
Bill Hall
Mary Jane McCaffrey Kelly
Tim Kulina
John Landis
Mike J. Rafferty
Mike P. Rafferty
Sarah Resick
Phyllis Rodgers
Ray Rodgers
Paul Smith
Jim Thomas
Tom Toner
Deb Waterkotte

Also, thanks to Cyla Alcantara, Nicolette Armstrong, Joe Bosco, Susan Brown, John DeMay, Paul Demilio, Sandie Earnest, Alan Friedman, Russell Gibbons, Arlene Girty, Bernie Hartman, Philip Jenkins, Steve Kolina, Cy Kulina (Thanks, Mum!), Lisa Mitten, Mike Murray, Rob Ruck, JoAnn Schipani, Carol Thorsen, and Preston Webb.

Thanks to Scott Bradley Smith for his editorial expertise and his never-ending patience and encouragement.

Special thanks to George Swetnam. ♦

To order additional copies of *Millhunks and Renegades: A Portrait of a Pittsburgh Neighborhood*, send $14.95 plus $1.50 postage and handling ($3.75 in Canada) for each book to Brandt Street Press, P. O. Box 8243, Pittsburgh, PA 15217-0243. Or order online at www.brandtstreetpress.com. ♦